Susanne Martin
Dancing Age(ing)

Susanne Martin (Dr.) researches, performs, and teaches contemporary dance. She focuses on improvisational approaches to performance making, narrations of the ageing body, contact improvisation, and practice as research/artistic research. Her solos, collaborative works, mixed evening formats, lectures, and workshops are presented internationally. She studied dance at Rotterdam Dance Academy, Folkwang University, Inter-University Centre for Dance Berlin, and holds a PhD from Middlesex University London.

Susanne Martin
Dancing Age(ing)
Rethinking Age(ing) in and through Improvisation Practice and Performance

[transcript]

Bibliographic information published by the Deutsche Nationalbibliothek
The Deutsche Nationalbibliothek lists this publication in the Deutsche Nationalbibliografie; detailed bibliographic data are available in the Internet at http://dnb.d-nb.de

© 2017 transcript Verlag, Bielefeld

All rights reserved. No part of this book may be reprinted or reproduced or utilized in any form or by any electronic, mechanical, or other means, now known or hereafter invented, including photocopying and recording, or in any information storage or retrieval system, without permission in writing from the publisher.

Cover layout: Kordula Röckenhaus, Bielefeld
Cover illustration: Lars Åsling, »The Fountain of Youth«, Göteborg, 2013
Printed and bound in Great Britain by Marston Book Services Ltd, Oxfordshire
Print-ISBN 978-3-8376-3714-4
PDF-ISBN 978-3-8394-3714-8

Contents

Foreword | 9

Introduction | 13
Dance and Age | 13
Research Context | 15
Approaching Dance through Improvisation | 20
Critique as/in Practice | 21
The Mixed Materials of this Research | 24
Chapter Outline | 32

I. A Dancer's Perspective and Approach | 35
Introduction | 35
Artistic Background and Perspective | 35
Research Approach | 46
Summary | 58

II. Understanding Age(ing) in Age and Dance Studies | 59
Introduction | 59
Introducing Age | 59
Approaching Age(ing) through Age Studies | 63
Intersections of Age Studies and Dance Studies | 75
Summary | 87

III. Improvising Age(ing) | 89
Introduction | 89
Building Microstructures for Sustained
Artistic Practice | 90
Dealing with Physical Constraints | 98
Preparing the Ground for Rethinking Age(ing) | 109
Summary | 121

IV. Performing Age(ing) | 123
Introduction | 123
Negotiating Age(ing) in Current
Performance Making | 124
Performing Age(ing) – A Performance Practice | 138
Summary | 160

Conclusion | 163

Works Cited | 173

ONLINE VIDEO COLLECTION DANCING AGE(ING)

Please go to: https://vimeo.com/album/3144399
Password: Dancing Age(ing)

Documentation of Performances
Clip 1: The Fountain of Youth (55 min)
Clip 2: The Fountain of Youth – Trailer (4 min)
Clip 3: The Fountain of Age (32 min)
Clip 4: The Fountain of Age – Trailer (4 min)

Documentation of
Practical Studio Research – Solo Partnering
Clip 5: Walk & Talk (10 min)
Clip 6: Placing Body Parts in Space (14 min)
Clip 7: Be Obvious (15 min)
Clip 8: Autumn Leaves (9 min)
Clip 9: Dress (11 min)
Clip 10: What I'm Good In Now (4 min)
Clip 11: Private or Performance (18 min)
Clip 12: Shift (6 min)

Documentation of Rehearsal Process
Clip 13: Rehearsal Fountain of Youth (9 min)
Clip 14: Rehearsal Fountain of Age (13 min)

Interviews
Clip 15: Kirstie Simson (16 min)
Clip 16: Andrew Morrish (20 min)
Clip 17: Katarina Eriksson (46 min)
Clip 18: Julyen Hamilton (43 min)
Clip 19: Ray Chung (58 min)

Artistic Responses to Age(ing)
Clip 20: Rosalind Crisp (28 min)
Clip 21: Andrew Morrish (19 min)
Clip 22: Ray Chung, Katarina Eriksson, Susanne Martin (18 min)

Foreword

This book is the outcome of my doctoral research in the field of contemporary dance. From the perspective of a dance artist I look at experiences, narratives and practices of age(ing) that are specific to this professional field. Across the chapters of this book I discuss how in particular dancers who focus on improvisation shape their careers in ways less prone to dualistic stereotyping and (self-)discriminatory age(ing) narratives, which dominate our culture as a whole. Additionally I analyse strategies in performance making that enable representations of age(ing), which collide with, resist, and 'ambiguate' normative expectations of age(ing). In other words this book is about the specific potential of dance to do and to represent age(ing) differently. In this way I hope to inspire the currently developing discourse on age(ing) in dance. I further support motions in the field that allow dance to grow up and to become a critical artistic practice of and for all ages. Last but not least I aim to make the knowledge and strategies developed in dance available for a broader critical age(ing) discourse.

I embarked on the journey of doing a doctorate with the particular knowledge and the reflective tools I developed as a dance artist, driven by the desire to do research while continuing to be a dancer. The decision to engage with academic research as a dancer led me to spend a few years moving my body back and forth between dance studios, university seminar rooms, and all kinds of spots where I could plug in my computer. It also led me to move back and forth between the UK, where I received funding and supervision for a Practice as Research PhD, and Berlin, which is my artistic home.

As a result, *Dancing Age(ing)* is a multi-modal Practice as Research investigation. It can be seen as an example of the recent inclusion of artists and artistic approaches into academic research. What in the UK context is termed Practice as Research and Artistic Research in Scandinavia and Continental Europe is an exciting, controversial shift in the relationship between artistic practice and academic knowledge production. Practice as Research opens up vibrant discussions about artists' modes of developing new ways of knowing in relation to academic questions around methodologies and epistemologies. In the case of *Dancing Age(ing)* this means that alongside written text the research is articulated through the original performance works *The Fountain of Youth* and *The Fountain of Age* and a documentation of the research process, all made available through an online video collection.

What is true for the modes of rethinking age(ing) in and through dance is also true for the modes of doing a Practice as Research inquiry:
Dancing Age(ing) is just one way of doing it.
There are more ways.
And there are more ways to come.

Many people have contributed to the project as a whole and I am very grateful for their input and intervention. Thank you to those artists who generously shared their knowledge and experience in interviews and artistic responses: Ray Chung, Rosalind Crisp, Katarina Eriksson, Julyen Hamilton, Andrew Morrish, and Kirstie Simson. Thank you also to the artists who shared the practice of Solo Partnering with me: Mamen Agüera Pérez, Mireia Aragonès, Shannon Cooney, Eliane Hutmacher, Andrea Keiz, Brigitte Kießling, Fenia Kotsopoulou, Christine Mauch, Andreas Müller, Giorgia Minisini, Meltem Nil, Gabriele Reuter, Brenda Waite, Nina Wehnert, I Ying Wu, and Sabine Zahn. Thanks to Tanzfabrik Berlin for providing me with studio space. Thanks to Eliane Hutmacher for helping me to set my performances *The Fountain of Youth* and *The Fountain of*

Age. Thanks to Andrea Keiz for her advice and help in documenting this research. Thanks to all those who helped craft *Dancing Age(ing)* either by commenting and discussing with me or by proofreading parts of this text throughout its progression: Katharina Debus, Barbara Driesen, Rebecca van Es, Dimitra Frangos, Andrea Keiz, Heike Kleffner, Paula Kramer, Carla MacDougall, Crosby McCloy, Margie Medlin, Andrew Morrish, Zara Morris, Sybille Müller, Ralf Müller von der Haegen, Claudia Sikora, and Olaf Stuve. I would like to extend a special thanks to my supervisors, Jane Bacon at the beginning of the research and Lesley Main towards the end, and most of all to Vida Midgelow, who supported and challenged me throughout this entire process. This project was made possible by generous funding from the University of Northampton and Middlesex University London. Thank you.

Introduction

DANCE AND AGE

Dancing Age(ing) examines contemporary Western dance and questions of ageing in this specific cultural and artistic context. The research builds on the premise that dance holds a multi-layered position in relation to age and ageing. Western theatre dance has often focused on youthful physicality and, as such, takes part in an unquestioned marginalisation of older bodies. According to the work done in age studies (e.g. Kathleen Woodward 1999, Margaret Morganroth Gullette 2004, Valerie Lipscomb and Leni Marshall 2010) this attitude is indeed pervasive in Western culture more generally.[1]

A number of studies also show that the majority of professional dancers transition out of their performance careers in their early to mid-thirties (William J. Baumol, Joan Jeffri, David Throsby 2004, Cornelia Dümcke 2008, Barbara Dickinson 2010, Mindy N. Levine 2005, Elisabeth Schwaiger 2012, and Steven P. Wainwright and Bryan S. Turner 2006a, 2006b). However, dance, and specifically

---

1 | I use the terms 'Western dance' to delineate my discussion to be about a European and North American lineage of artistic dance and 'Western culture' referring to the broader culture in which this kind of dancing and my overall discussion is embedded. However, I invite the reader to acknowledge the problematic nature of this term. As Stuart Hall so clearly analyses in The West and The Rest (1996: 184-227) 'the West' is also a simplifying, generalising concept that homogenises differences within Western cultures and, even more severely, it is one that takes part in constructing non-Western societies as the inferior other.

contemporary dance, is also a site for questioning and inventing new ways of experiencing and presenting human bodies in movement (e.g. Adam Benjamin 2010, Teresa Brayshaw and Noel Witts 2014, Raimund Hoghe 2005). To locate these discussions it is useful to clarify that I understand contemporary dance not as a specific dance style but as a "notoriously fluid" descriptor (Martha Bremser and Lorna Sanders 2011: xv) of the multiple moves, aesthetic directions, and interests in Western artistic dance that have developed since the early twentieth century. The common denominator of this multiplicity is the will "to challenge the expectations and sensibilities of the public or to present unsettling images of contemporary life" (Deborah Jowitt in Bremser and Sanders 2011: 2) and, especially since the 1960s, "the capacity to reflect critically on its various enterprises and to choreograph commentary about its own artistic process" (Susan Leigh Foster 1986: xx).

In turn, contemporary dance also has the potential to question or dismantle stereotypical body and age-related values and images that are not only a part of dance but also our everyday culture (Ann Cooper Albright 1997, Lipscomb and Marshall 2010, Janice Ross 2009). The ways in which this potential can be realised, and indeed, is already being realised is the subject of this book. It primarily addresses how contemporary dance and improvisation (as a crucial practice within contemporary dance) can contribute to a critical discourse on age(ing). Furthermore, it asks which processes in my own artistic practice enable such critical engagement. How can what I call an 'age critical dance practice' be conceptualised and realised?

As a whole the research is based on a deconstructive understanding of age, which I discuss in Chapter II. However, to initiate a clarification of the terminology employed in this text I address in this Introduction some key terms and related concepts, beginning with 'age(ing)'. My understanding of the term 'age(ing)' is influenced by the writings of the German age researcher Miriam Haller, who works with the terms 'Alter(n)' and 'Alter(n)sstudien' (2005, 2009,

2010a).[2] Though the use of brackets in her work emphasises that her field of inquiry is not limited to old age, I see the use of brackets in the context of my research as a stumbling facility, thus rendering the often-used word 'ageing' unfamiliar. Indeed, the brackets accentuate that ageing is the gerund of age. As such, they show that ageing is not a special and closed period in life but rather a continuum. I suggest that the brackets open up the word ageing towards multiple meanings.

The specific understanding of age(ing) advanced in this research draws primarily on a body of theoretical work established in the field of age studies. A main objective in this field is to demonstrate that age, together with class, race, and gender, is one of "the most salient markers of social difference" (Woodward 1999: x). Consequently, critical age researchers are concerned with "understanding how differences are produced by discursive formations, social practices and material conditions" (Woodward 1999: x), as well as establishing a critical age consciousness throughout a whole culture, across all disciplines, and for all stages of life. Thus age studies question our everyday understanding of age(ing) and, in the context of this research, serve as a theoretical foundation for reconsidering the implications of the commonly agreed youthfulness of dance. Furthermore, insights gained by age studies buttress my interest to develop an artistic practice that exposes, questions and subverts stereotypical representations of age(ing) bodies.

RESEARCH CONTEXT

This study considers age(ing) from the perspective of contemporary dance, a specialist area of professional art practice with particular ecologies and economies of practice. It does not discuss age(ing) and dance from the point of view of dance science, medicine, or other applied perspectives, which might consider, for example, "the impact

---

2 | 'Alter' translates as age and 'Altern' translates as ageing.

of dance on health and well-being among older people" (Mary Kate Connolly and Emma Redding 2010: 1). Furthermore, my approach does not include research on dance practices and dancers in relation to training efficiency, injury prevention or injury treatment such as the studies carried out by the National Institute of Dance Medicine and Science, UK and the International Association for Dance Medicine & Science (IADMS) to name just two of the leading institutions for such research.[3] The scope of the research further excludes the field of community dance. Although community dance recognises and supports dance as an activity for all ages and abilities, it generally understands dance as an amateur activity facilitated by professionals to "contribute positively to self-worth, self-confidence and a sense of wellbeing" (Diane Amans 2008: 6). As dance researcher Nanako Nakajima, who has analysed understandings of age(ing) in both professional theatre dance and in community dance, explains:

> In Community Dance, the postmodern idea that anyone can dance is interpreted as social inclusion. Dance scholar Sara Houston formulates that socially excluded participants will be empowered through Community Dance and set themselves on a road to a better life. (Nakajima 2011:100)

Rather this book concerns itself with the field of professional dance and focuses on the perspectives of its practitioners. Existing research on the work realities of professional dancers, for example a study focussing on eleven Western countries initiated by the International Organization for the Transition of Professional Dancers (IOTPD), shows that "although [dancers] thought they could continue until their late thirties, on average they actually stopped dancing professionally in their early to mid-thirties" (Baumol, Jeffri, Throsby 2004: 4). Most dance performers are therefore in their twenties and those who still perform in their forties and beyond continue to be ex-

---

3 | For more information on dance science and dance medicine see: http://www.danceuk.org/healthierdancer-programme/dance-medicine-and-science-research/; http://www.iadms.org/; http://www.tamed.de

ceptions in the wider field of Western professional dance. However, this research emphasises that the 'empirical youthfulness' of dance should not be regarded as naturally given, but is instead the result of a complex cultural, social, and economic reality, that deserves further analysis and critique.

Thus this specific discussion of age(ing) in dance needs to be understood in the context of the macrostructures of the professional dance field. Macrostructures are what I call the complex mix of institutionalised funding, curating, and dissemination structures in relation to the organisational modes through which artists realise their work. Or, more abstractly, macrostructures are the cultural-discursive, material-economic, and social-political orders that shape current dance practices.[4] Two aspects of the current macrostructures in the contemporary dance field impact particularly on questions of age(ing). The first aspect is the hierarchical distribution of power, which is a defining feature of dance companies, or any highly institutionalised dance organisation. The second concerns the independent dance field and could be called the unequal distribution of attention or encouragement for dance makers of different ages. Both constrain the ways in which specific dance practices can unfold and age(ing) dancers can sustain their place in the professional field.

According to the evaluation of the above-mentioned IOTPD study, the most realistic opportunities for performers to earn a living with dance is within established company structures (Levine 2005: 11). However, the company as the provider of a relatively reliable income is bound to hierarchic structures. Despite the diverse ways dance companies are organised, what is important in relation to age(ing) is the typical division of labour between choreographer

---

4 | Stephen Kemmis, Jane Wilkinson, Ian Hardy and Christine Edwards-Groves, who carry out research in the field of contemporary practice theory offer a substantial analysis of how the cultural-discursive, material-economic, and social-political as 'practice architectures' prefigure and shape practices (Kemmis ed.al. 2014: 43).

(as author) and dancer (as interpreter or co-choreographer). This division constricts a dancer's agency regarding decisions such as who can continue dancing and for how long. Company dancers usually cannot extend their careers beyond their mid-thirties and do not have the decision making power to change this professional trajectory. In cases in which companies support dancers to continue past their mid-thirties, this is still a top-down decision and the dancers' agency in shaping their work reality according to personal needs remains limited.[5]

Whilst the structures of the independent sector have a less decisive relationship to age(ing) they are not unproblematic either. In this context artists individually define and deal with the way they integrate their temporal and continuously age(ing) bodies into their artistic productivity. They tend, according to dance and performance theorist Bojana Kunst, to be positioned as entrepreneurial performer/author/manager of their own artistic productions, realising their art with the aid of artist networks and art mediators in series of projects (Kunst 2009, 2012a, 2012b, 2012c). However, ageism[6] also has an impact the on independent dance sector through what I have above referred to as the unequal distribution of attention or encouragement for dance makers of different ages. Even more directly than company dancers, freelancing dancer/choreographers have to offer their dancing bodies, their concepts, and their performance-works to the art market and try to succeed in terms of funding and visibil-

---

[5] | Two prominent examples of companies with or especially for older dancers are the Nederlands Danstheater III (1991-2006 under the direction of Jiri Kylian) and Wuppertaler Tanztheater (directed 1973-2009 by Pina Bausch).

[6] | 'Ageism' was first coined by physician and gerontologist Robert Neil Butler in 1969, and commonly refers to negative discriminatory practices against old people, but can also describe prejudice, stereotyping, and discrimination of other age groups such as children or adolescents. Ageism also includes "process[es] of implicit aging self-stereotypes" (Levy and Banaji 2002: 62).

ity. Yet, according to Kunst (2012a), support structures for freelance and project-focused independent artists tend to re-establish youthfulness in dance, in the ways they stereotypically equate something new with youth, and the category youth with progressive or innovative. I propose that these notions uncritically mirror our overall age(ing) culture (discussed in Chapter II). As a result, support structures are established that try to foster and educate young talents, and provide attention and public visibility to 'emerging' artists. Kunst offers an illuminating explanation of such an ageist undercurrent in her analysis of the independent dance sector as one that, as a whole favours work that is "young", "new" and not yet realised (2012a: unpaginated). She describes the independent dance field as one marked by constant production, distribution, and sale of what she calls "art-to-be" (Kunst 2012b: unpaginated). This dynamic is hardly feasible for older artists with a record of previous artistic outcomes and an artistic practice that already defines their public image. These artists cannot and might not want to repeatedly represent a promising and unencumbered potential. They do not fit the imagination and expectations of an art market that aims to support fresh, raw talent, hoping to turn it into great art and economic success in an unknown future. To be sure, this is not an argument against supporting young artists, but against narrowing down the possibility of 'new' to a specific age group, and for questioning more thoroughly what it is we are looking for in the 'new' and 'young'.

Against the backdrop of these macrostructures of contemporary dance, the dancers addressed and cited in this book can be seen to have created artistic works, practices and strategies that take part in doing and representing age(ing) in ways that have the potential to shift the established ways of thinking and dealing with age(ing) in dance (addressed in Chapters III and IV).

Approaching Dance through Improvisation

My discussion of age(ing) and dance places a special emphasis on improvisation, not as an artistic category in opposition to choreography but, as dance scholar and artist Vida Midgelow notes (2013), as a central approach within contemporary dance making. This focus is inspired by the observation that a significant number of dancers who developed improvisation as a source of dancing, as an inquiry into composition, and as a performance practice in the 1960s, are still performing. These dancers are now well into their 70s or beyond, and include Simone Forti, Anna Halprin, Deborah Hay, Steve Paxton, and Yvonne Rainer. Their continuing presence suggests that their specific practices have been able to accommodate the changes of their age(ing) bodies. It could be argued that their practices allow them to keep testing and exploring dance through and for their own bodies, thus in a way freed of a static idea of an 'appropriate' dance body or age limit.

Or, put differently, Paxton's contact improvisation, Forti's logomotion, Rainer's choreographies of 'unspectacular' movements, Halprin's healing rituals, Lisa Nelson's tuning score(s), and Hay's solo dance scores all served to bring about new virtuosities in dance that do not rely primarily on youthful athleticism. The relevance of these artists in terms of our understanding of dance practice, choreography and performance making has been acknowledged for example by Sally Banes (1987 and 1995), Melinda Buckwalter (2010), Ramsey Burt (2006), Susan Leigh Foster (1986 and 2002), Friederike Lampert (2007), and Cynthia J. Novak (1990).

My research acknowledges that the specific improvisation practices of all these artists and their continued visibility as performers have shifted the parameters of what dance is and could be in terms of its relationship to age. Similar to and inspired by Janice Ross' discussion of Anna Halprin's late works (2007) and the interviews collected by Fergus Early and Jacky Lansley in *The Wise Body* (2011), I argue that this and later generations of dancers, who include improvisation, experimentation, and openness to change into their approach to dance making, and who continue to dance and perform into old age, have developed artistic works, practices, and alternative virtuosities that can serve as fertile ground for rethinking age(ing) in and through dance. Indeed, this argument is additionally supported by the significant number of internationally acclaimed dance artists now in their 50s and beyond. For example, Julyen Hamilton, Eva Karczag, Mark Tompkins, or David Zambrano place a strong focus on improvisation in and as performance. But also for performers such as Liz Aggiss, Jonathan Burrows, Raimund Hoghe, Wendy Houstoun and La Ribot, for whom improvisation is not necessarily a performance practice, improvisation plays a central role in the process of performance making (see Chapters III and IV).

In many ways, improvisation is also the foundation of my artistic making as a contemporary dancer, thus providing another reason to focus on it as a key practice in this investigation of dance in relation to age(ing). In my own dance practice improvisation offers a frame of reference and a technical base. It is sometimes used as a mode of artistic inquiry, and sometimes as its subject. I therefore define my own dance practice as improvisation-based. My rethinking of age(ing) in and through dance in this inquiry is further shaped and formed by my concept of 'age critical dance practice', to which I will now turn.

CRITIQUE AS/IN PRACTICE

Although age studies is a field that critically studies age, 'age critical' as a term has not yet been established in age studies. Nonetheless, some scholars, such as Gullette, already refer to themselves as 'age critics' (2004: 5). Drawing from this, I position an age critical practice as a perspective or approach that questions dominant ideas on age, such as the opposing of youth to age, both of which are assumed as fixed categories. Taking an age critical position rejects such dualities as the foundation for researching age, and instead makes such dualities one of the objects of analysis. Thereby, in this book, the term age critical signifies the attempt to "provide new critical tools for the understanding of the aging process" (Heike Hartung and Roberta Maierhofer 2009: 16), and to "allow for subversive deconstruction of normative age concepts" (Ulla Kriebernegg and Maierhofer 2013: 17). The term, therefore, is not in disagreement with the definitions and terms established in age studies. Rather, it is a grammatical construction that allows me to depart from the existing discourse and speak about dance as my main object of study with a perspective informed by (critical) age studies. In other words, it allows me to develop and speak about the concept and the potential of 'age critical dance practice'.

My decision to highlight the term 'critical' is also influenced by philosopher Michel Foucault's understanding of critique (1997). As philosopher and gender theorist Judith Butler writes: ""critique" is precisely a practice that not only suspends judgment for him [Foucault], but offers a new practice of values based on that very suspension" (2001: unpaginated). In Foucault's own words critique would read for example as: "a political and moral attitude, a way of thinking, etc. [...] which I would very simply call the art of not being governed or, better, the art of not being governed like that and at that cost" (2007: 45). In line with Foucault and Butler, I understand age critique as a practice and, therefore, as an ongoing process that is both personal and in relation to the social world. It is the process of suspending normative judgement about age(ing). This entails working towards a perception of age that suspends a fixed sense of truth about age(ing), in this specific case in its relation to dance as an art form.

To be sure, the Foucauldian concept of critique has been applied in several interesting ways in dance studies. Dance theorist Pirkko Husemann offers an in-depth discussion of choreography as a critical practice in her analysis of the works of Xavier Le Roy and Thomas Lehmen (2009), while theorist Gabriele Klein argues for dance theory to be a practice of critique (2013). While Husemann's discussion revolves around choreographers whose artistic working methods and outcomes can be read as immanent critique of the established norms and modes of production in the current dance field, Klein develops her concept of critique to argue against the traditional practice/theory divide.

Similar to these discussions, this study focuses on how the field of contemporary dance, and more specifically how the individual participants in this field including myself can avoid reproducing norms of age(ing), and instead can take part in producing alternative imaginations, concepts and practices regarding age(ing) in dance. Or, from a Foucauldian perspective, an age critical position in dance means developing the art of not being governed by detrimental age norms.

Against this background, my inquiry into age critical dance practice is inspired in particular by the research of Elisabeth Schwaiger. Her work is significant since she was the first researcher to specifically address the relationship between current Western theatre dance and age(ing) while using the critical theoretical framework of age studies (2005a, 2005b, 2006, 2009, 2012). Though her approach is an important contribution to this otherwise neglected relationship, two significant gaps remain. Firstly, Schwaiger's research is informed primarily by the Australian dance context, which, according to Schwaiger, is much more ballet-oriented than European or US-American contemporary forms of dance. Consequently her analysis of the contradictions and struggles of midlife[7] dancers cannot be fully applied to current European discourses and aesthetics in contemporary dance. Secondly, Schwaiger's main focus is to theorise the relationship between dance and age in terms of subjectivity,[8]

---

7 | In psychology, sociology, and gerontology the term midlife refers roughly to the period between age 40 and 64, following early midlife and giving way to old age. The term midlife has replaced the previously more common term middle age.

8 | The term subjectivity refers to the long standing and multiple philosophical discourses on a human sense of self or individual self-understanding of what it means to be a subject or a conscious doer. Subjectivity is further addressed in Chapter II.

rather than illuminating the specific details of dance practice. As such, her research concludes by identifying promising approaches towards "a mature subjectivity" (Schwaiger 2005b: 118) inside the field of "experimental dance practice" (Schwaiger 2012: 25), which corresponds with what I would call improvisation-based dance.[9] Yet it is outside the scope of her work to trace the actual artistic processes, working structures and bodily doings of such practice in their critical potential. My research aims to fill such gaps. I argue that for a shift in the discourse on age(ing) in dance to occur, it is necessary to investigate and further develop practices, processes and actual performances that match what Schwaiger roughly labels 'experimental dance practice'. In doing so, this artistic research inquiry tries to take part in contradicting, shifting, or, with reference to Butler (1993) and Shannon Sullivan (2000), imperfectly reiterating embodied norms or views on both dance and age(ing).

THE MIXED MATERIALS OF THIS RESEARCH

Until this point I have introduced *Dancing Age(ing)* in terms of its questions and ideas. However presenting ideas through the medium of a written text is only one part of this doctoral dissertation. Other parts employ the medium of theatrical performance and video documentation.

---

9 | I read Schwaiger's use of the word 'experimental' in the context of her discussion of dance styles with a ballet orientation versus less codified approaches to dance. In the former, dancers aim at reproducing a preset bodily and choreographic scheme, while in the latter exploration of movement ideas, detailed perception of one's own body in movement, and the possibility of artistic decision making emphasise dance as an experimentation through and about individualised movement. As such the characteristics of experimental dance conform to an improvisatory approach in/to dance.

Introduction 25

Performances

The Fountain of Youth (2013) and The Fountain of Age (2015)

Photos: Lars Åsling, William Gillingham-Sutton

Two solo performances constitute the arts-practical outcome of this research, as they articulate my specific propositions of how to rethink age(ing) in and through improvisation practice and performance in an artistic fashion. The solos *The Fountain of Youth* and *The Fountain of Age* were presented live for a general audience and two appointed PhD examiners at Middlesex University on 5 November 2014 and 18 June 2015. Both pieces explore critical narratives and representations of age(ing). They aim at a general audience and address age(ing) through a collage of scenes in which dance, text, costume, mask work, and music interrelate in such a way that ambiguity, discontinuity, and irony support the audience's critical reflection on age(ing).

Both pieces are humorous in tone and generate a playful atmosphere of deconstructing age(ing) by blurring fact and fancy, artifice and informal, improvised and pre-set movements, irony and empathy, dancing and lecturing, the personal and the fictional. They work with ambiguity as a central strategy to disrupt any closed or one-dimensional meaning of age(ing). The scene *Improvisation & Dementia* for example (in *The Fountain of Youth*) explores and exposes moments of disorientation akin to dementia as a vital element of creative and improvisational processes. The scene *The Doc Martin Forever Young Meta Method* plays with messy, unsophisticated moving as a subversive strategy against an omnipresent call for staying fit and young and the convention of age appropriate, self-controlled behaviour in midlife. Since such theatrical outcomes are of an ephemeral nature, this book gives access to a video documentation of these live events (clip 1-4). Thus video constitutes the third medium through which *Dancing Age(ing)* is articulated, even though it is important to note that videos cannot substitute the inherently time and site bound performances (Adam L. Ledger, Simon Ellis, Fiona Wright 2011). In this sense, the performance videos only document the performative outcomes of this research, providing a valuable account of the artistic component of this project. Furthermore, the video collection includes the following selection of clips that give insight into the Practice as Research process.

Solo Partnering

Solo Partnering at Tanzfabrik Berlin 2012-2014, video stills

The video clips 5-12 feature the improvisation practice of *Solo Partnering*, which was central to my approach. The selection of eight clips provides insight into what happens in a dance studio during this specific solo improvisation practice, what this practice looks like, how it operates, and what questions and reflections arise. *Solo Partnering* is discussed in Chapter I and III.

Rehearsals

Rehearsals The Fountain of Age (2014) and The Fountain of Youth (2013) at Tanzfabrik Berlin, video stills

Clip 13 and 14 provide examples of the solo rehearsal processes in the making of *The Fountain of Youth* and *The Fountain of Age*. They show the particular stage of searching for scenes and images that, in the end, form the solo pieces.

Interviews

From the left: Simson (2013), Hamilton, Martin (2011), interviews, video stills

In the videos 15-19 the dance artists and improvisation experts Ray Chung, Katarina Eriksson, Julyen Hamilton, Andrew Morrish, and Kirstie Simson reflect on their work and careers in relation to age(ing). The data from the interviews and the artistic responses (see below) importantly inform my discussion of improvisation and performance making in Chapter III and IV.

Artistic Responses to Age(ing)

From above: Crip (2012), Morrish (2014), Eriksson, Chung, Martin (2014), artistic responses, video stills

Introduction   31

Three clips (20-22) present what I call *artistic responses to age(ing)*. In the process of approaching artists with questions about age(ing) I developed modes of acquiring information that allowed my interview partners to make use of their dancing bodies and their improvisation skills, instead of just relying on a standard interview. The clips contain artistic responses by Rosalind Crisp, Andrew Morrish and a trio between Ray Chung, Katarina Eriksson and myself.

It is important to note that there is no necessary order to approach these sources. Just as the performances attempt to be accessible (i.e. to be understood without having read the book), also the text aims, as much as possible, to be accessible without previous knowledge of the performances and the practice documentation contained in the video collection. However, my writing is partly based on these sources and from time to time refers to specific clips. I suggest that it is only through watching the *Fountain* pieces[10] and other examples of the Practice as Research processes that the physical, visual, compositional dimensions of the research become perceptible. Given that dance does not translate fully onto the page, for the written part I highlighted certain aspects of what is ultimately a multi-dimen-

---

10 | To avoid extensive repetitions of fully naming the titles of the two solos that form part of this study, I will at times refer to them as the 'Fountain pieces'.

sional project. Since the written text cannot disclose all dimensions of my artistic practice the experience of the work itself is vital, even if only viewed by way of video documentation. Through this, one can gain insight into the way I dance, compose, and relate to the audience and what kind of ambiguities and deconstructions of age(ing) I create and confront my audience with as a dancer.

Furthermore, one can find unique and relevant material on the practice of improvisation in the *Solo Partnering* and rehearsal excerpts, as well as in the clips with interviews and artistic responses, which could be especially useful for further research on improvisation.

Chapter Outline

Chapter I, entitled *A Dancer's Perspective and Approach*, provides information on my artistic background and research perspective as an improvisation-based dance maker and relates this to the specific approach of Practice as Research in the arts. It then gives an overview of the methods developed and employed, such as the gathering of expert knowledge on improvisation and age(ing) and the documented studio research practice *Solo Partnering*. Together these methods allow for an artist and artistic practice oriented examination of how dance can contribute to a critical discourse on age(ing).

Chapter II, *Understanding Age(ing) in Age and Dance Studies*, expands on age theory and relates it to current discourses in dance studies and dance practice. Based on cultural constructionist and deconstructive feminist discourses on age(ing) I understand age(ing) as enculturated. This approach has enabled me to discuss how dance participates in our current 'age(ing) culture' and how it can expose different ways of "doing age" or "undoing age" (Haller 2010b: 216).

Chapter III, *Improvising Age(ing)*, discusses the potential of improvisation as an implicitly age critical practice and mainly draws on my engagement with a number of improvising artists as well as on my own particular improvisation practice. The chapter argues that artists who focus on practicing improvisation have developed strategies and working structures that shun the repetitious construction of what, in age studies, is discussed as the expected, desired and 'normal' youthful (fit and virtuous) body and the actual body as its 'other', more inadequate companion. Several aspects of improvisation as a reflexive self-practice are discussed that support the individual and serve the age(ing) artist in continuously (re)defining the parameters of her[11] dance making.

Finally, Chapter IV, entitled *Performing Age(ing)*, examines performance making and how it enables dance to articulate an explicitly age critical position. It draws on examples and voices from the current dance field as well as my performances *The Fountain of Youth* and *The Fountain of Age*. This last chapter mainly argues that reflexive and critical performances of age on stage/in artworks question age stereotypes and allow alternative representations of age to gain visibility.[12] Based on my own performance works, the chapter seeks to strengthen the notion of ambiguity in performance as a strategy to challenge and deconstruct dualistic understandings of youth and age in dance and beyond.

---

11 | Throughout this text I chose to exclusively use feminine pronouns in situations where the referent could be any gender.

12 | The construction 'performances on stage/in artworks' here emphasises deliberate artistic performances for an audience as opposed to habitual and less conscious performances in everyday life, which are discussed for example by Judith Butler with the term 'performativity' (1993: 2-23) or by Pierre Bourdieu with the term 'habitus' (1984: 169-175).

I. A Dancer's Perspective and Approach

Introduction

This chapter locates this study in terms of its research perspective and approach. Both aspects are interconnected and are grounded in my specific practice of improvisation-based dance making. The chapter begins with a short review of my artistic background, situating the perspective applied as that of a contemporary dance artist. What follows is a discussion of Practice as Research as my principle approach and an identification of the two main methods employed. In the discussion I trace the development of these methods, both improvisation-based, throughout the research. Together they facilitate an investigation of the relationship between dance and age(ing) as well as the development of a new perspective on dance's age critical potential.

Artistic Background and Perspective

My research perspective can be placed in the context of contemporary dance, one that no longer actively negotiates a ballet tradition, be it positive or negative, but is instead grounded in a twentieth century Western dance tradition. Within the broad field of contemporary dance, I define my own mode of practicing and producing dance as improvisation-based.

Improvisation

Since the very beginning improvisation has been an integral part of my dance education and development, starting in my childhood in 1973. The wide range of teachers I had over the years brought their unique approach and information to my current understanding of improvisation-based dance making. Until 1994 the teachers with whom I studied improvisation were mainly based in a European dance tradition, with an explicit reference to the work of Rudolf von Laban and Mary Wigman. Especially influential was my very first teacher, Ulla Weltike-Bilitza, who was educated in part by Else Lang (1906-1999), a student of Mary Wigman. Her teaching integrated technical training, improvisation, and the making of new dance works. Accordingly, the concept of dance I grew up with between the ages of five and fifteen was that dancing and learning to dance is made up of the following:

- Exploring tasks, themes or musical qualities through improvisation
- Learning set movement materials provided by the teacher
- Employing a mix of both approaches in long-term choreographic processes in which all groups of the school worked on their specific scenes and roles for a full evening dance theatre piece performed every second year

During my professional education at the Rotterdam Dance Academy, the Netherlands (now known as Codarts) I specialised to become a teacher for modern dance and improvisation. It was during this training that I first began to use improvisation as a form in its own right. At the academy, I studied improvisation with Els van Buren, Hilke Diemer, and Ciel Werts. All three taught improvisation based on a specific curriculum, which was developed in the Netherlands in 1968, and called *Dansexpressie* (dance expression). *Dansexpressie* can be defined as "a form of dance in which the elements of dance (body, effort, time, space) are dealt with creatively and inspiration becomes visible in a personal movement language" (Diemer 1990: 13, my translation from Dutch). The development of *Dansexpressie* at the Rotterdam Dance Academy has its roots in Laban's movement studies and in the didactic concepts of the school's founder Corrie Hartong (1906-1991), also a student of Mary Wigman, and her colleague Kit Winkel (1916-2003) (Diemer 1990: 10, Hartong 1985).[1] My subsequent teachers in improvisation and contact improvisation were part of or influenced by those artists who have been performing improvisation on stage in the USA since the 1960s. Ray Chung, Simone Forti, Julyen Hamilton, Lisa Nelson, Kirstie Simson, Nancy Stark Smith, and David Zambrano, to name a few, have provided me with invaluable information as teachers. I deliberately contextualise my dance practice through naming the individual artists who influenced it and avoid the categories of Ausdruckstanz, modern dance, postmodern dance as well as a clear distinction between improvisers and choreographers. Too easily the assumed definitiveness of those terms brushes over the complexity of conceptual and personal differences, and also the connections between the artists mentioned above.[2]

---

1 | From 1992-1994 I also studied for two years at Folkwang School in Essen, Germany (now Folkwang University). This school, founded by Kurt Jooss, is another influential dance education in continental Europe, based in early modern dance, which kept working with and further developing its specific dance heritage. Interestingly, at the time of my studies improvisation was not cultivated, neither as part of the modern dance classes nor as a subject in its own right. Correspondingly, in Rotterdam improvisation in the form of *Dansexpressie* was exclusively offered to those studying to become teachers, not to students of the stage dance branch.

2 | Simply put, the term modern dance describes the new artistic dance movement in Europe and North America between 1900 and 1960. Ausdruckstanz or expressionistic dance is often used to describe German modern dance roughly from the beginning of World War One to the end of World War Two. Postmodern dance then refers the body of work of North American dance artists since the 1960 whose works did not continue the

Just as different sources and people inform my dancing beyond fixed categories, the same goes for the works of each of these artists. The interviews of dancers collected in the book *The Wise Body* (Jacky Lansley and Fergus Early 2011) are a compelling example of how dancers are influenced by each other, by history, political and social conditions and by the experience of moving between continents, aesthetics, and bodies of knowledge. When, for example, Bisakha Sarker, a performer of creative and classical Indian dance, talks about Uday Shankar, in whose school she studied in Kalkutta, she sheds light onto an overlooked part of twentieth century transcontinental and transcultural dance history. Before starting his academy for music and dance 1938, Shankar danced extensively in the USA and Europe in the 1920s and 1930s, first with the ballerina Anna Pavlova, later with his own company, mixing elements of Indian and Western dance traditions (Sarker in Lansley and Early 2011: 162). Sarker also points to improvisation as an approach to dance that has a history and relevance beyond European and North American dance forms. "Then there was a fourth class, which we called general class, where we learnt the Uday Shankar style. This was actually an improvisa-

---

aesthetics identified with modern dance. The critique of these terms as analytical categories is in itself a rich and ongoing discourse in dance studies. See exemplary Banes' new introduction to her book *Terpsichore in Sneakers* (1987: xi-xxxix, first edition 1980). Here she acknowledges to have revised her understanding of modern dance and further develops her definition of postmodern dance. Subsequently, Burt, in the introduction to his book *Judson Dance Theatre* (2006: 1-25), provides an explicit critique of Banes definitions and questions understandings of expressionism, modern and postmodern dance in US American discourses more generally by way of discussing "transatlantic crossings" (2006: 1) between European and US American dance works. Enriching for the ongoing discourse on the concepts underlying these terms as well the term contemporary dance, which I use in this book, is also the critique articulated from a postcolonial perspective. See for example: *Breakin' the Rules* by Rachel Fensham (2013) and *Worlding Dance* edited by Foster (2009).

tion class. That is why I feel very uptight when people say there is no improvisation within Indian dance culture" (Sarker in Lansley and Early 2011: 161). Personal dance histories such as Sarker's underscore the complexity of artistic lineage and the limitations of categorisations in dance, be it temporal, geographical or aesthetic.

Similarly, my own development as improvisation-based dancer and performance maker draws on more complex relationships and sources than on those teacher-student experiences acknowledged above. Of major importance for my personal dance making are my peers, colleagues and friends, with whom I have practiced and performed throughout the years. They each have not only supported my development and growth as an artist, but also have influenced the specific trajectory of this research. Those I collaborated most with include Katarina Eriksson, Eliane Hutmacher, Andrea Keiz, Bronja Novak Lindblad, Gabriele Reuter, and the German theatre group *Theater M21*.

Performance Making

My current artistic practice comprises of a range of doings or subpractices. I practice and teach solo, group, and contact improvisation and also research and train within a range of more codified movement practices like yoga, ballet, or contemporary dance trainings. I create solo performances as well as collaborative works such as the performance series *Susi & Gabi's Salon*, conducted together with Gabriele Reuter.[3] I also perform in directed theatre works, as with

---

3 | In *Susi & Gabi's Salon*, conceived and conducted together with Gabriele Reuter, we present dance and performance with changing guest artists, and induce dialogue between the artists and the audience mainly revolving around questions of improvisation. Gabriele Reuter is a dance artist and urbanist who collaborates with other dancers, photographers and musicians. See also: http://www.gabrielereuter.de/

Theater M21.[4] My work with *Theater M21*, under the direction of Joachim von Burchard deserves a special mentioning in understanding how my performance tools and strategies are not only informed by European and North American dance traditions, individual dance artists, and an emphasis on improvisational practices. Working as a performer/actress with *Theatre M21* influenced and sharpened many elements of my current performance aesthetics. *Theatre M21*, with which I realised ten original theatre pieces since 2001, can be placed in a post-Brechtian theatre lineage in Germany, for which theatre scholar Hans Thies Lehmann coined the term 'postdramatic' (2006). Working with this theatre company has expanded my performer strategies and dramaturgical tools and has provided me with tools to include text and character work in my own performance making. It has helped me developing a performance practice that combines immediacy and open attention as practiced in dance improvisation with my appetite for irony, parody and theatrical narration. In terms of performance style, my own current mode of post-dramatic performing relates to a Brechtian tradition insofar that I am presenting a performer's attitude that keeps a critical distance to the activities performed and employs what in Brechtian terms is an anti-illusionist *Gestus des Zeigens*, an obvious attitude of showing (Bertolt Brecht 1963: 281-284).[5] Another feature my style shares with much postdramatic or postmodern performance practices is the tendency to make the means and mechanisms of theatrical making transparent, such

---

4 | Information on this ensemble, albeit only in German language, is available at: http://joachimvonburchard.de/arbeiten.html

5 | "Zeigt, daß ihr zeigt! Über all den verschiedenen Haltungen / Die ihr da zeigt, wenn ihr zeigt, wie die Menschen sich aufführen / Sollt ihr doch nicht die Haltung des Zeigens vergessen [...] Und hinter euren / Figuren bleibt ihr selber sichtbar, als die, welche / Sie vorführen." (Bertolt Brecht 1963: 281-284). Show that you show! In all the different attitudes you show when you show how people behave/perform you should not forget the attitude of showing [...] And behind your characters you stay visible as the one demonstrating/performing them (my translation).

as visible costume or mask changes, occasional communications with the sound or light technician or visibly operating myself the stage technical equipment.[6] What is shared then, is the interest in producing images and situation of intentional ambiguity in which it is impossible to distinguish with certainty what is fiction, what is real, what is skilfully improvised, set, or accidental.

Obviously, my artistic background, which is roughly portrayed here, and my stylistic preferences as well as my experiences of teaching, being directed, improvising, or setting performances all collaboratively inform and influence my artistic practice. However, not all of my artistic activities are explicitly employed for this research. As already indicated in the Introduction, the practice I foregrounded during the inquiry is my performance oriented solo improvisation practice *Solo Partnering*, which I developed as one of my central practical research methods. The other practice I developed further in and through this research is my performance practice *Performing Age(ing)*.

What I call *Performing Age(ing)* is my engagement with creating pieces, mostly solo works, that clearly deal with age(ing), a topic I began to address in 2003. Defining *Performing Age(ing)* as improvisation-based specifies the performance making process used, whilst also differentiating my approach from what might be called 'performing improvisation'. While I sometimes explicitly perform improvisations, in *Performing Age(ing)* I use the tools and methods that I developed through my long-term engagement with improvisation, and the images and imaginations acquired during *Solo Partnering* to create distinguishable theatre pieces with a set narrative and drama-

---

6 | The aesthetic positions collected under the term postdramatic are not fundamentally different from those discussed in theatre and dance studies under the label postmodern. The conceptual difference lies in the fact that the term postdramatic aims at keeping the contextualisation of the artistic objects and practices under scrutiny tightly related to the history of European theatre, rather then to the much broader field of postmodern and poststructuralist theories (Karen Jürs-Munby in Lehmann 2006: 13-14).

turgy each. The following brief description of the main works – *Herr K. Müh, Claudia, JULIO, and Rosi tanzt Rosi* – which both precede and inform *The Fountain of Youth* and *The Fountain of Age*, depict *Performing Age(ing)* as a long-term performance practice. The prevailing mood of these pieces is humorous. They work with parodic elements and a quotational use of popular music from different times as a rich tool for playing with multi-layered age and time references and codes from everyday (mass mediated) life.

Herr K. Müh (2003) is a solo piece in which I perform a male character in his early sixties in a moment of life-review and upheaval. *Claudia* (2004) is a solo work that presents a female 'best ager' eager to try out new things. The songs of Julio Iglesias figure in both pieces and his oeuvre of Latin pop songs subsequently form the leitmotiv in *JULIO – The Group Version* (2006) and *JULIO – The Solo Version* (2006). *JULIO* explores questions of gendered age(ing). It revives the solos *K. Müh* and *Claudia* and juxtaposes both with a video work and a photo exhibition. Furthermore, the *Group Version* features a performance-lecture on gender by Olaf Stuve[7] and live versions of Julio Iglesias songs sung by Eliane Hutmacher.[8] *Rosi tanzt Rosi* (2007-2009) is a body of work comprising many different performances that centre on the fictional dancer Rosi, who appears in the pieces in different ages and stages of her life. This series, which also constitutes my MA research project, examines, amongst other things, the collision between age(ing) and a pronouncedly feminine dance repertoire. In 2013 and 2015 these performances where followed by *The Fountain of Youth* and *The Fountain of Age* (clip 1-4) as the latest articulations of *Performing Age(ing)* (the *Fountain* pieces are further discussed in Chapter IV).

---

7 | Olaf Stuve is a sociologist who specialises on queer and critical masculinity studies, intersectionality, gender-reflective pedagogy, and neo-Nazism prevention. See also: http://dissens.de/gerenep/english.php
8 | Eliane Hutmacher is a dancer, and dance pedagogue focussing on improvisation-based approaches to performance making with young adults. See also: http://www.alte-feuerwache.de/academy/

I. A Dancer's Perspective and Approach   43

Furthermore, specific attention to the performer-audience relationship is always an important element of each work. Therefore, in addition to my strong base and ongoing engagement with improvisation, my specific audience approach, laid out in the following, can be regarded as another defining aspect of my dance practice.

Hosting an Audience

In my performances I explore a relationship between performer and audience that involves reciprocity and complicity. It can be understood as a host-guest relationship, similar to the situation at a dinner or a party. The awareness of the possibility of such a host-guest relationship and the wish to develop hosting in my own performance work is informed by several sources. Firstly, there is the particular audience approach of the Théâtre du Soleil, founded and directed by Ariane Mnouchkine, whose work I first saw in the 1990s (Le Tartuffe, 1995 and Et Soudain des Nuits d'Eveil, 1997). Letting the audience see the make up and costume preparation before the show, as well as a shared meal during the break, were essential elements of the performances. In watching these pieces I felt like a guest in their workplace, yet a guest who could benefit from the specific ethics and aesthetics they were developing and collectively realising.[9]

Moreover, the performance maker Bronja Novak Lindblad[10], with whom I have performed since 2001, has influenced me with her disregard of any formal distance between herself and her audience. She shows no need for a moment of privacy or time to transition between presenting her dance work and casual, private conversation with members of the audience after a performance. I often

---

9 | It would exceed the scope of this book to expand upon the seminal work of *Théâtre du Soleil*. A good introduction gives Judith G. Miller's book *Ariane Mnouchkine* (2007).
10 | Bronja Novak Lindblad creates pieces for adult and children audiences, mixing dance, music and drama. See also: http://bigwind.se/forestallningar/barn-unga/birollen-och-musikanten/

experienced how she gravitates towards the audience instead of the dressing room at the end of the applause. She enjoys the direct and if possible uninterrupted contact to her audience in a way a host would enjoy conversation and a sense of community with her guests after having cooked and shared her new favourite dish.

Last but not least, the performance practice of improviser Andrew Morrish[11] influenced my interest in hosting. In his view, as I understand it, an audience's distance, incomprehension or alienation towards new performance works stems partly from not feeling included or considered but merely confronted with a performance. Morrish's has an interest in laying the ground for staging improvisation by being in tune with the audience (or 'breaking the ice') before the performance starts. Consequently, in formal as in informal performance contexts he makes it part of his improvisation to receive and welcome his audience.

My audience approach has developed along these lines of influence. My personal take on hosting often includes directly addressing the audience, which often gives a light and ironic tone to the performance. Regularly, I reveal the curiosities or questions that gave rise to the specific performance in order to offer a rather specific context and focus to my audience. My particular way of hosting tries to strike a balance between giving too many and too little clues on the nature of the shared experience, that is my performance, so that both my guests and I can relax and assume some degree of common ground. In the series *Susi & Gabi's Salon,* I continue to explore and refine my tools for hosting to create a dialogue and a shared reflection on questions of dance improvisation. The series is born out of a discontentment that my Salon-partner Gabriele Reuter and I have as performers and as an audience of improvisation. In the role as either performer or audience member we often experience an unhelpful gap between the complexity of what happens for and between the

---

11 | Andrew Morrish is a performer, researcher, facilitator, and teacher of improvisation. His performance work currently focuses on solo improvisation. See also: http://www.andrewmorrish.com/

performers and what the audience of dance improvisation is able to grasp and decipher. As *Salonnières,* or hostesses of a Salon, we explore strategies to make the process of improvisation more accessible and support the audience experience at an improvised performance. We develop playful communal scores and structures for sensitising and opening up our sensory and imaginative receptivity. We explore how much and what contextual information is helpful. We also facilitate and encourage a verbal sharing of ideas, intentions, observations, and association between all people present.[12] Thus, the term hosting describes my ongoing engagement with questions of sharing and inviting into an aesthetic experience. This significant characteristic of my practice can as well be seen in this research's video documentation. It determines the specific style in which I conduct the interviews, invite for artistic responses, or record my *Solo Partnering* sessions. In all these activities I address the reality of the recording video camera and make explicit its function as connector and mediator to a future audience. I host my dance or interview partners as well as the virtual audience and in this way make them accomplices in this Practice a Research. At the end of Chapter IV I return to the notion of hospitality and how I apply it in *Performing Age(ing)* as an element of my age critical performance making.

In summary, the rough synopsis of my artistic background and some important characteristics of my current practice serve to specify my positioning as improvisation-based contemporary dance art-

---

12 | In the Salon program notes our intention is articulated in the following way: "Susanne Martin & Gabriele Reuter (Berlin) revive a European tradition that dates back to the 17th century; a salon is a gathering of people under the roof of an inspiring host (Susi & Gabi as Salonnières do their best to inspire!), held partly for amusement and partly to refine taste and increase the knowledge of the participants through conversation. In dialogue with invited guests and the audience, these evenings revolve around the phenomenon of improvisation as performance, choreography and research" (Martin 2011). See also: http://www.susannemartin.de/category/salons/

ist. It outlines the field or network of artists from which I chose my participants and informants for this study. It delineates the specific performance practice for this research on age(ing) as one that has been informed by my long-term engagement with improvisation while not aiming to present performances of improvisation. Instead, it aims to develop and set images and narratives that address age(ing) critically. The way I employ and further develop my particular improvisation-based practice in and for this research directly reflects the main argument of this book. I argue that by engaging in improvisation practice dancers can critically and reflexively explore the ever-changing realities of their always age(ing) dancing bodies, while in performance more explicitly age critical images and narratives can be offered and shared with an audience.

Research Approach

The Introduction to this study already made clear that although this research project articulates my particular perspective this in no way means that I research exclusively my own modes of practice. Rather, drawing on a range of sources, I also discuss the unique perspectives, writings, and works of artists who have realised what I call explicitly age critical performances. Furthermore, to find out about what I call the implicit age criticality of improvisation I engage with a range of expert practitioners of improvisation.[13] Drawing on my particular perspective and knowledge as artist, however, does mean that the way I approach these other artists, and how I formulate my research questions, are rooted in the tools, methods, and sensibilities of an improvisation-based dance maker. The particular ways of collecting or creating research data are indeed influenced by an artistic approach to searching, finding, and organising information.

---

13 | I draw here on the terms 'arts-disciplinary expert practitioner', 'expert practice', or 'expert performance making' as discussed by dance scholar Susan Melrose (2005, 2007).

In other words, improvisation practice and my improvisation-based performance making has both informed this project's emerging methods. In the following sections I discuss what this means in detail, first in terms of Practice as Research as my overall approach, second in regard to the methods developed and employed, which demonstrate how my artistic tools and strategies are constitutional for the research design of *Dancing Age(ing)*.

Practice as Research

My research approach builds on an understanding of Practice as Research as a domain of research "in which the practice of art – that is, the making and the playing, the creation and the performance, and the works of art that result – play a constitutive role in a methodological sense" (Henk Borgdorff 2007: 21). Recent publications on the subject of Practice as Research in the performing arts by Jane Bacon and Vida Midgelow (2010), Estelle Barrett and Barbara Bolt (2007), John Freeman (2010), Baz Kershaw and Helen Nicholson (2011), and Robin Nelson (2013) respectively show that the goal is to activate and share artistic processes that can be critically reflected and discussed rather then to create empirically grounded formulas of art making. According to Kershaw and Nicolson, an important characteristic of current research methods in theatre/performance studies more generally also appears to be the case in the Practice as Research approach in *Dancing Age(ing)*: namely that the "relationships between the researcher and the researched are often fluid, improvised and responsive", and aim at "the cultural production of flexible research ecologies wherein tacit understandings, inferred practices and theoretical assumptions can be made explicit and can, in turn, be queried and contested" (Kershaw and Nicolson 2011: 2). Specific to Practice as Research, as formalised inside Higher Education in the UK, is that one or several 'pieces' of artistic practice are "submitted as substantial evidence of a research inquiry" (Nelson 2013: 8-9). In my case the solo performances *The Fountain of Youth* and *The Fountain of Age*, presented live for examination and included as a video documentation, constitute this evidence.[14]

In my Practice as Research process, to paraphrase Bacon and Midgelow, I entered into a dialogue with my emerging movement materials and my creative research process developed through its own logic of improvisation practice and performance making. In this way the knowing/knowledge developed and embodied in the inquiry "is not simply a demonstration of a pre-theorized intellectual position but an explication of its own internal discourse that can be understood via its intersection with other varied discourses" (Bacon and Midgelow 2010: 12). Practice as Research in this undertaking is used to create a productive spiral (Sondra Horton Fraleigh and Penelope Hanstein 1999: 76), one in which my researcher's quest for new insights on age(ing) and my dancer's experience in practical experimentation have moved me forward. The vantage point of a researcher allowed me to seek out and articulate the age critical potential of dance by finding intersections with critical age discourses. At the same time, the artistic experimentation had an impact on and changed my reflective and theoretical engagement with current age discourses. This allowed me to further develop the potential in my own practice. However, while I argue that Practice as Research is productive, its complexity is difficult to handle, if only because the particular logics and the necessary rigor of dance practice and academically accepted researching and writing practice each tend to demand full-time engagement. Nonetheless, at the end the research spiral of *Dancing Age(ing)* has resulted in an articulation of a new artistic/research perspective on the relationship between age(ing) and dance. It is an articulation that could not have developed by academ-

---

14 | Nelson (2013) provides a comprehensive overview of the history and current discourses of Practice as Research in the Arts in Higher Education in UK und beyond. The journal *Choreographic Practices*, edited by Bacon and Midgelow, partakes in the ongoing discourse on Practice as Research by publishing articles about dance practices as mode of research. http://www.intellectbooks.co.uk/journals/view-Journal,id=170/

ic discussion of already existing dance practice or through creating new and original work alone.

The Methods of Dancing Age(ing)

Building on Jennifer Parker-Starbuck and Roberta Mock's discussion of methods in performance research (2011: 211), my methods are routes to encounter bodies and practices, including my own, tools to collect evidence and information, and means to gain deeper understanding about how dance can participate in a critical discourse on age(ing). Thus the research developed as it went through different phases. Initially it was guided by the more general hypothesis that improvisation as a specific approach within contemporary dance holds inherent properties that enable and attract dancers to continue performing as a life long practice. This in turn led to two modes of inquiry. Firstly, I was interested in knowing how expert improvisation practitioners experience and respond to age(ing). Secondly, I wanted to investigate my own improvisation practice in terms of its relationship to age(ing). This two-pronged approach defined the research methods of this project, that is, my performative interviewing of improvisation experts and my explorative inquiry into and through my own improvisation practice *Solo Partnering*. The use of these methods was consistent throughout the research phase. Yet my understanding and concrete use of both methods shifted in the course of the inquiry. It is to this last point that I now turn.

Performative Interviews on Improvisation and Age(ing)

In retrospect my method of gathering expert knowledge on the relationship between improvisation practice and age(ing) can be described as a trajectory that started with semi-structured interviews that followed guidelines for conducting qualitative interviews in social research (Kathy Charmaz 2006, Jaber F. Gubrium and James A. Holstein 2001, Tom Wengraf 2001) and concluded with inviting improvisers to perform for me *artistic responses to age(ing)*. Indeed, at the beginning of the research process I decided to interview a range of experienced and still actively performing improvisers (mainly those over the age of 50), whose improvisational practice I perceive to be close to my own in many ways, such as in approach, technique, aesthetic or direct influence/lineage (as outlined above). When choosing the research participants, my familiarity with the work of these artists was central. This familiarity enabled a certain degree of mutual trust, respect and artistic understanding. From the perspective of the interviewee, both a dancer's lived and embodied idiosyncratic art making and her experience of age(ing) are intimate and could make her feel vulnerable for being misunderstood.[15] From my perspective as a researcher it was vital for me to be able to ground my analysis of these artists' verbal articulations in an actual embodied understanding of the multi-dimensional practice that give rise to the words.

Accordingly, my interpretation of how these age(ing) artists perceive and respond to their individual age(ing) process in relation to their professional work is grounded in a range of sources. In addition to the recorded interviews and artistic responses, my analysis also relies on my participation in their workshops, attending their performances, and the knowledge I have gained from working with them in a number of professional contexts over the years. Specifically my data gathering concentrated on the following improvising artists: Ray Chung, Rosalind Crisp, Katarina Eriksson, Julyen Hamilton, Andrew Morrish, and Kirstie Simson.[16] During the main period

---

15 | The issue of vulnerability and inequity is obviously not bound to dancers as research participants, but part of any interview situation. It is therefore extensively addressed in the literature on interview methods as part of qualitative social research designs. See for example Charmaz 2006, Gubrium and Holstein 2001, Wengraf 2001.

16 | Ray Chung (born 1952) is a performer, teacher, engineer, and artist. He has worked with contact improvisation since 1979 and integrates other forms including martial arts, bodywork and Authentic Movement. See also: http://www.italycontactfest.com/insegnanti-2013/ray-chung/

of the research (2011-2014), I once again participated in their workshops and recorded their statements. To select the candidates from the practitioners with whom I am familiar, I used a typical improvisation strategy, i.e., I chose to focus on what presented itself to me at the time. In other words, I approached those artists whose paths crossed mine. Including someone like Lisa Nelson, for example, certainly would have enriched the project but the travel budget did not allow for it. Instead, I relied on serendipitous meetings, which mostly occurred in my hometown Berlin (all the meetings with artists with the exception of the initial interviews with Chung and Eriksson took place in Berlin). Moreover, letting go and accepting the ephemeral is another virtue of improvisation that I embraced for this project. In September 2011, for example, I conducted a full evening performance as part of my series *Susi & Gabi's Salon* with and about

---

Rosalind Crisp (born 1959) defines her artistic practice as choreographic improvisation. She works as soloist, collaborates with musicians, visual artists, and dancers, and choreographs ensemble works. See also: http://www.omeodance.com/

Katarina Eriksson (born 1965) is a performer and teaches contact improvisation and other improvisational forms in Europe and the US. Since 2000 she curates the performance series *Moments Notice* in Berkeley. See also: https://plus.google.com/+KatarinaErikssonIMPRO/about

Julyen Hamilton (born 1954) is a dancer, improviser, poet, musician and teacher who creates solo works, collaborates with other artists and directs the improvisation-based company *Allen's Line*. See also: http://www.julyenhamilton.com/index.html

Andrew Morrish (born 1951): see footnote in section 'audience approach' above.

Kirstie Simson (born 1958) is an improvisation dancer and teacher. Contact improvisation and Aikido amongst others inform her practice. See also the documentary on Simson, *Force of Nature* by Katrina McPherson (2012): https://vimeo.com/34894689

Amos Hetz.[17] During the performance we danced and talked about his relationship to age(ing) and to the art of improvisation, but most of the video recording later turned out to be corrupt. Accepting that I could not repeat this particular research-in-performance-moment, I let go and decided to trust other possibilities for gathering expert knowledge to come.

As I continued with my research I relied more and more on my improvisation-based tools for triggering, organising and composing my encounters with artists. While the first two semi-structured interviews with Chung and Eriksson (clip 17 and 19) in August 2011 followed a list of set questions informed by qualitative research designs, at a later date I started to explore more improvisation-led modes of gathering artists' ideas and knowledge. I took the risk of departing from the well reviewed and documented interview methods developed in other research areas to see what would happen when foregrounding and using my embodied knowledge as dancer and improviser in regard to collecting data. This approach resulted in the collection of research data by means of creating situations that tapped into the unique improvisation and performance expertise of each artist I encountered. Additionally, I allowed for modes of articulation that reflect each artist's particular practice as well as my own. This amended approach to using strategies emanating from performance making and from improvisation was not solely motivated by experimental curiosity about applying artistic strategies to research. In fact, it was also instigated by the first two interview experiences. The interviews with Chung and Eriksson confirmed the problematic status of verbal statements as reliable or 'true' representation of a persons practice and experience, which has been discussed at length by scholars doing qualitative research. Norman K. Denzin, a researcher on qualitative inquiry, puts it this way:

---

17 | Amos Hetz (born 1933) is a performer and movement teacher; he composes solo dances, dance-collaborations, and movement games. See also: http://www.amoshetz.com/

[T]here is no clear window into the inner life of a person, for any window is always filtered through the glaze of language, signs, and the process of signification. And language in both, its written and spoken forms is always inherently unstable, in flux, and made up of the traces of other signs and symbolic statements. Hence, there can never be a clear and unambiguous statement of anything including an intention or a meaning. [...] Experience, lived and otherwise, is discursively constructed. It is not a foundational category. There is no empirically stable I giving a true account of an experience. Experience has no existence apart from the storied acts of the performative-I. (Denzin 2014: 2)

Following Denzin's claim, I contend that there are no clear and unambiguous statements, but rather my research participants have articulated complex and volatile moments of performative self-construction. Building on Denzin's argument, any attempt to give the 'unstable and in flux' words of these artists more weight and value by tightening the interview method, could be seen as almost naïve. Accordingly, I chose to go in the opposite direction. Instead of trying to eliminate the social, the relational, and the temporal from the interview situation to achieve comparable, 'objective' or 'authentic' statements, I looked specifically for modes to value and foster the unique, volatile moments of performativity by setting up situations of actual doing, exploring, thinking, and playing.

For example, I designed the following meeting with Hamilton in December 2011 as a conversation, or an improvised duet (clip 18). In it I also offer my own reflections, raw and improvised wordings to keep 'passing the ball' between us, as in an improvised dance, in which the goal is not to hone the preconceived patterns of each but to see what arises from the instantaneous meeting of bodyminds. From there the endeavour of improvisation-led method creation moved to designing a performance score for the next expert. For Crisp, in January 2012 (clip 20) I prepared sheets with keywords that she could respond to associatively either through dance or words. I decided upon keywords that touch on my own curiosities as well as to possibly inspire her to move:

- Living and Dead Bones
- Beautifully Old – Beautifully Young
- Morbid Wisdom
- Experience that leads to … …
- Weakness, Stiffness, Tiredness
- Post Menopause – The Witch
- Career – Visibility – Recognition

In July 2013 I planned on doing something similar with Simson, but had to let go of preconceived ideas and trust the possibilities of the moment when, due to an acute injury, Simson was not able move (clip 15). Thus the encounter rather took the shape of a semi-structured interview. In April 2014 Morrish, in contrast, was offered the space for a 15-minute open score solo on age(ing) (clip 21). That same summer I met with Chung and Eriksson for a second encounter. I proposed a score for an improvised trio dance during which each has the possibility to step close to the camera to reconfirm or adjust their earlier statements from 2011 (clip 22). In October 2014 I completed collecting expert knowledge with a semi-structured interview with Morrish (clip 16). These details show how the improvisatory approach of recognising and working with the potentials of each moment, shaped this constantly evolving Practice as Research method. Or, as Morrish says: "[Improvisation] is not just a set of tools that you use to make the art. If you actually accept it as a performance form in its totality, then everything that is happening to you is the material. So as you change the material [and the research method] changes" (Morrish 2014, clip 16, min 4:20).

Exploring Age(ing) through Solo Partnering

In 2009 I initiated an improvisation practice format that I called *Solo Partnering*. It is a method to create and reflect upon dance improvisation as a performance practice. It also provides a peer-supportive microstructure to assist me and other improvisation-based performers to sustain creative practice throughout the shifting conditions of work and life. Since 2011, in the research process for *Dancing Age(ing)*, *Solo Partnering* was examined, used, modified, refocused, and documented in order to accommodate a dynamic artistic (self) exploration of the relationship between age(ing) and dance. To make this studio practice as comprehensible as my other central method of inquiry, it is again useful to trace this practice and its development during the research in more detail.

Solo Partnering is based on a structure for sharing practice that I learned from the solo improviser Morrish.[18] Through *Solo Partnering*, I investigate, develop and share my continuing interest in improvisation with a wide range of partners. The practice offers a framework for a peer-to-peer exchange that works through the intimate constellation of two dancers alternately performing for each other. During each *Solo Partnering* session, both partners train and clarify aspects of their improvisational dance skills, their methods, and work on their current artistic questions. Each partner is allotted an equal amount of time for experimentation, verbal self-reflection, and feedback on their solo making. Thus, this practice combines what Nelson terms 'know how' and 'know what'. The 'know how', in applying Nelson's discussion of arts practice to improvisation, is the tacit knowing of what works in and as improvisation, developed while improvising.[19] The 'know what' signifies the process of critical reflection on "the methods by which what works is achieved and the compositional principles involved" (Nelson 2013: 44).[20] The rigour

---

18 | I met Morrish for the first time in 2003 in Berlin. Morrish, the improviser Heide Moldenhauer and I engaged in an intensive period of practicing solo improvisation. It was the particular working structure that Morrish proposed and that we kept using during the two months of regular studio practice, on which *Solo Partnering* is based.

19 | Nelson draws here on the concept of 'knowing how and knowing that' developed by analytic philosopher Gilbert Ryle (2009: 14-48).

20 | Nelson's discussion of 'know what' draws on Donald Schön's work on 'reflection-in-action' (1983) and corresponds to my discussion of reflexivity in Chapter IV.

of critical reflective dialogue between the partners is vital in each *Solo Partnering* session.

At the beginning of this research, I decided to make this practice the site for the artistic explorative component of *Dancing Age(ing)*. This consequently changed the way I experienced the practice. The focus on age(ing) intensified my awareness of the complex relationship between the following: my day-to-day experiences of being and having a midlife body, my assumptions, values and aims as dancer, and the compositional questions that arise in solo dancing. A year into the research, I narrowed the practice focus. I decided to guide my improvisations during *Solo Partnering* explicitly and consequently towards age(ing) as subject matter for performing. Instead of only observing how a self-guided improvisational dance practice accommodates my always-changing body and circumstances of life I started to improvise 'about' age(ing). As a result the practice became a method to explicitly question and rethink age(ing) in and through my creative and physical practice. While the principals and the structure of supportive peer exchange stayed intact, and my respective partners could still follow their own artistic agendas, *Solo Partnering* transformed into a method to search, find, produce or allow for multiple associations, narratives, and imagery on age(ing) in and as performance. Finally some of the imaginative representations and narratives of age(ing) developed during *Solo Partnering* were selected, shaped into two solo performances and presented as artistic outcome of this research (for further discussion of *Solo Partnering* see Chapter III).

Documenting Processes – Processes of Documentation

The mixed mode nature of a Practice as Research approach necessarily increases the significance of documentation. As I already outlined in the introductory chapter, *Dancing Age(ing)* employs more than just one mode of articulation. Alongside text, two public live performances are presented as outcomes of the research. Furthermore a video documentation is included that helps to articulate and evidence the inquiry. The video footage collected in this documentation includes "integral documentation" as well as "external documentation" (Angela Piccini cited in Ledger, Ellis, Wright 2011: 166). While the two staged *Fountain* performances are external documentations, filmed by the professional videographer Dominique Rivoal (clip 1-4), all other videos are integral documentations, carried out myself with the simplest means and as tools of the research (clip 5-22). The external documentation of the final performances allows for access to the artistic outcomes of the research, which otherwise could not be shared beyond the live event in the theatre. Videos of interviews, artistic responses, and of my solo improvisation process are part of the integral documentation processes and imperative to realising the research. These video-documents comprise the core data of my research. The integral documentation enabled a process of observation, recognition, remembrance, and reflection vital for the general objective of rethinking age(ing) in and through my improvisation practice and performance making. Finally, including some of this material in the accompanying video collection means that the methods developed and employed, as well as the overall multidimensional research process, are made transparent and thus open for criticism and evaluation.

I argue that the development of these methods confirm the potential and necessity of Practice as Research to work with idiosyncratic methods that draw from and speak to the particular research context, that are, as it were, custom built for a particular research project. In other words, my methods stay intentionally close to artistic practice yet also become productive for a Practice as Research approach, which is built on the intention to weave together and let unexpected resonances occur between the gathering of expert knowledge, first-person creative inquiry, and performing, to gain deeper understanding about how dance can participate in a critical discourse on age(ing).

SUMMARY

The preceding chapter situates my position as a dance researcher in terms of my own artistic background in improvisation-based dance. It further discusses Practice as Research, as established in UK academic research culture, as the overall research approach of *Dancing Age(ing)*. This is followed by a review of my two main research methods, which are firstly a particular and emergent mode of collecting expert knowledge on improvisation practice and age(ing) through interviews and artistic responses, and secondly the first-person artistic exploration of my own improvisation practice *Solo Partnering*. Finally, the chapter addresses the role of documentation in this Practice as Research project. The next chapter will turn to the theoretical framework of *Dancing Age(ing)*, thereby deepening the conceptual discussion of age(ing) that I started to explore in the introduction of this book.

II. Understanding Age(ing) in Age and Dance Studies

Introduction

In this chapter I continue with some of the discussions I first addressed in my introduction. The chapter delves into the meaning of the term age and I offer my personal age autobiography as an example of the complexity of the term and how it plays out in a dancer's life. The second part of the chapter explores the discourse of age(ing) that can be found in age studies. The chapter concludes with a discussion of age(ing) discourse in dance studies, one that is currently gaining momentum. My focus on theorising age(ing) provides relevant analytical tools for the practice-led discussion of the age critical potential of improvisation and performance making that follows in Chapters III and IV.

Introducing Age

Examining the meaning of 'age' reveals a complex net of normative categories that informs our everyday understanding of the term. Age scholar Woodward disentangles the term by differentiating between six definitions of age stemming from very different fields. She speaks of 'chronological age', 'biological or functional age', 'social age', 'cultural age', 'psychological age' and 'statistical age' (2006: 183). As will become clear, each of these age definitions is distinctive and influential. Together they function as interlinked albeit contradictory categories. Starting with chronological age, it refers to the number of years one has lived, counted through each completed year after one's officially registered date of birth. Secondly, one's biological or functional age is derived from a medical perspective on age. Biological age is determined by physiology rather than chronology and concerned with rating one's state of health and physical capacity. Somebody with a severe disease would be categorised as functionally much older, meaning being closer to death, than someone of the same chronological age in a better physiological state. Social age, as a third possible classification, characterises the meaning a society attaches to different age-categories through their legislation and social politics, determining one's function and role in society. Here strong markers are, for example, one's legal age and one's age of statutory retirement. Although both are linked to a specific chronological age, they are clearly subjected to societal negotiation processes and, therefore, historically contingent. As a fourth definition of age, Woodward works with the idea of cultural age, which she states is similar to social age in that *"cultural age* refers to the meanings or values that a culture assigns to different people in terms of age, but here status and power are crucial" (Woodward 2006: 183). Cultural age is concerned with the interest one raises, or the expectations and wishes projected onto the individual. Though not specified in numbers and not officially negotiated as social age, it is a very powerful normative mechanism related to the cultural orientation towards youthfulness that, according to many age theorists, permeates Western culture as a whole. Psychological age, the fifth definition, is concerned with self-perception in regard to age, thus pointing to how old one feels. Finally, statistical age refers to "predictions concerning age based on large data sets" (Woodward 2006: 183). The last definition derives from the world of demography and epidemiology and is concerned with, for example, comparing life expectancies of different populations.

Indeed, in much of the writing on age(ing), social and cultural age are conflated and discussed as the social or socio-cultural perspective on age. For the purpose of *Dancing Age(ing)*, however, the differentiation is more helpful. That is because dance is an explicit cultural intervention without direct relation or influence on social politics and legal regulation. For this reason the focus of this present study leans on Woodward's definition of cultural age. In the following, I apply Woodward's categories to help create my personal age autobiography, which underscores the complexity of dealing with age as soon as an individual life is taken into consideration.

The idea of rewriting one's age autobiography is one of the most important concepts Gullette has developed in her critical writing on age(ing) (Gullette 2004, 2011). I take together Woodward's age categories and Gullette's biography approach to ensure that my dancer/researcher involvement with the subject is more accessible and, moreover, to point to the field of professional dance as one with its own cultural specific relationship to age(ing):

At the time of writing this age autobiography my 'chronological age' is 45, which does not say much about my age at the moment different audiences read this chapter. My 'functional age' on the most general level is relatively young, given that no life threatening diseases or impairments show up on my medical record. On a more detailed level I suffer from injuries and weaknesses of the musculoskeletal system, which points towards an age difference between my left metatarsal and, for example, my very functioning kidney. In regard to my teeth, even the biological and functional definitions seem to diverge. As two complete rows of teeth are in use I can speak of 100 per cent functionality. However, some of them are prostheses, which means that biologically only 75 per cent of my teeth are alive. All of this does not say anything about a tumour I might have, which has not yet been discovered. Moreover, all the non-life threatening illnesses that have shaken my body in regular irregular waves since I can remember have always insisted that well-being and strength are not a continuum, not even in childhood or youth. 'Legally' my age has not changed since I turned eighteen and I will keep that age until my death or the moment someone certifies me to be of unsound mind. I was rated old enough for dance at the age of five by my parents and by dance teachers. When I finished secondary school at the age of nineteen, I was, ac-

cording to state funded dance institutions in Germany, already too old to start a professional education. Luckily I learned that other countries see things differently and I went to study dance in the Netherlands. The last few years I have been a university funded PhD researcher in my mid-forties and I am thankful for the anti-ageist funding policies in UK. In my home country Germany the widely agreed age limit to receive funding for a PhD is thirty. Yet, 'culturally', my lifestyle, dress code and financial situation all fit the category of a student under the age of thirty. From a 'statistical' perspective my life expectancy increases with each year I live and I take part in raising the statistical age limit for active dancers with each year that I fill in my social security/tax declaration using the term 'dancer'. My 'psychological age' is flexible and shifting but since I started to become a dancer I often felt much older then I looked. I see this particular self-perception as related to three circumstances specific to the field of professional dance. Firstly, having danced throughout my entire childhood and youth I have a very long and rich practice history, and I will soon celebrate my fortieth stage anniversary. This produces a kind of veteran self-image. Secondly, I went through an 'age-socialisation' (Gullette 2004: 12) of being always already too old, or soon too old for dance. Thirdly, since my mid-twenties I regularly experience my body as failing, as vulnerable, unpredictable, painful, exhausted. My injuries, through their local specificity, produce a sense of fragmentation, of having several functional ages, of being an ambiguous patchwork of sensation and of states of health. Exhaustion, in contrast, when it affects physically, mentally and emotionally feels exactly like the symptoms commonly attributed to old age: reduced vitality, slower movement, slowed reaction time, and any activity is arduous. Yet my energy level continues to change as well as the age policies that surround me. For the time being I can only remain curious as to how my age autobiography will continue to evolve into the future.

This age autobiography should not be understood to offer the full story of my dance life or my experiences of age(ing). Neither does it aim to give a complete account of all the applications of the six age categories I can possibly find in my biography. What I try to bring to the fore with such narrative exercise is that these diverging views on age cannot be separated when trying to address age(ing) biographically. None of them alone would suffice to describe the complex story of age(ing). Furthermore, such a biography, when for example staged as a monologue, is an example for what I call performing age(ing) ambiguously. The multiplicity of perspectives taken articulates age(ing) as complex and ambiguous. Narrating or performing a biography in this way 'ambiguates' and consequently contradicts dualistic understandings of youth and age, health and illness. It renders the perception of age ambiguous not only for myself but for my audience. The idea of ambiguity, as discussed in age studies, will be picked up again later in this chapter. Ambiguity as a strategy for age critical performance practice will be further discussed in relation to my performance making in Chapter IV.

APPROACHING AGE(ING) THROUGH AGE STUDIES

To date, the subject of age(ing) in dance has not received much attention inside the field of dance and performance studies, although its relevance is starting to be recognised. As a result, my theoretical scrutinising of age draws on discourses established in the field of age studies (e.g. Gullette 1988, 1997, 2004, 2011; Haller 2009, 2010a, 2010b, 2011; Schwaiger 2005a, 2005b, 2006, 2009, 2012; Aagje Swinnen 2012, 2013; Woodward 1991, 1999, 2002, 2006) rather then dance studies. By addressing some of the questions raised and theories explored in age studies, my research aims to develop a deepened analytical understanding of the contradictions and potentials of dealing with age(ing) in the field of dance. Furthermore, insights from age studies support my research in developing an artistic practice that exposes, questions and subverts stereotypical representations of age(ing) (addressed in Chapters III and IV).

As such, my research on the relationship between dance and age follows the assumption that dance operates not only inside, but also mirrors and has the potential to speak back to its wider socio-cultural context. Dance follows and/or foreshadows changes in how to think about our bodily being and our age(ing). Dance plays a part in the negotiation and the performance of what is identified as old or young, just as it takes part in the negotiation and performance of what is female and what is male.[1] This assumption is useful for it locates the problems as well as the potential of rethinking age(ing) in dance as part of a wider discussion on cultural constructions on age in contemporary society. In turn, the approach to conceptualise and critique age(ing) in its cultural constructedness can be placed in a longer tradition of deconstructing and denaturalising social systems, norms, and identities.

The concept of deconstruction used in this chapter and throughout the book is based on the philosophical work of Jacques Derrida. Deconstruction challenges the dichotomies and hierarchies characteristic to concepts and philosophies based on oppositions. Examples of oppositions subjected to deconstructive critique are for example: nature and culture, mind and body, inside and outside, male and female, speech and writing. As Derrida suggests in *Signature Event Context*:

An opposition of metaphysical concepts (speech/writing, presence/absence, etc.) is never the face-to-face of two terms, but a hierarchy and an order of subordination. Deconstruction cannot limit itself or proceed immediately to neutralisation: it must, by means of a double gesture, a double science, a double writing, practise an overturning of the classical opposition, and a general displacement of the system. It is on that condition alone that deconstruction will provide the means of intervening in the field of oppositions it criticizes. (Derrida 1982: 329)

In other words, concerning age(ing), deconstructive approaches to analysis and practice are interested in "what is deemphasized, over-

---

[1] | Gender constructions, in contrast to age, have been much discussed in dance studies. See for example: Banes 1998, Burt 1995, Alexandra Carter 1996, Jane Desmond 2001, Alexandra Kolb 2009, Midgelow 2007.

looked, or suppressed in a particular way of thinking" (Jack M. Balkin 1995-96:2) about age(ing). Moreover, it asks what the hierarchies and subordinations in particular representations and discourses of age(ing) are. Deconstruction is most often discussed in relation to the written text and as a strategy of literary criticism. However, in an interview with Peter Brunette and David Wills, Derrida objects to confining deconstruction "to matters of language" and emphasises that "most effective deconstruction is that which is not limited to discursive texts" (Brunette and Wills 1994: 14-15).

Accordingly, critical analyses of age regularly draw on what can be called deconstructive concepts such as Butler's performativity (Haller 2010b, Schwaiger 2006, 2012, Woodward 2006), Pierre Bourdieu's habitus (Wainwright and Turner 2006a, 2006b; Schwaiger 2012, 2006),[2] and Foucault's concepts around subjectivity (Christopher A. Faircloth 2003, Schwaiger 2012, 2006). In simple terms, the concept of performativity by Butler describes how identities, in particular gender identities, are not naturally given but socially constructed through reiterated acts, doings, or "incessant activity performed, in parts without one's knowing, without one's willing" (Butler 2004: 1). Much of her work focuses "on the question of what it might mean to undo restrictively normative conceptions of sexual and gendered life" (2004: 1). Also sociologist Bourdieu theorises and deconstructs individual practice and conduct. For example, his concept of habitus denaturalises individual taste, comportment, and dispositions, and his empirical research proves these personal and deeply internalised features to be typical of and conditioned by one's position in the social space, such as class or milieu, and thereby functioning to reproduce social difference and inequality. Foucault, by contrast, concentrates on "creating a history of the different modes, by which, in our culture, human beings are made subjects" (Foucault 1982: 777) and on "the history of subjectivity", which he analyses as "the formation of procedures by which the subject is led to observe himself,

---

2 | Bourdieu's work differs from that of Butler, Foucault, or Derrida in so far as his perspective is sociological not philosophical.

analyse himself, interpret himself, recognize himself as a domain of possible knowledge" (1984: unpaginated). Hence my discussion of age(ing) in dance, which draws on the current discourses in age studies, is contextualised by broader philosophical discourses and intellectual lineages of poststructuralist, cultural constructionist and deconstructive feminist theories.

In particular, the specific range of questions raised by age studies become clearer through a reference to two early texts on age that have been influential in the formation of this field. The first text is Simone de Beauvoir's *The Coming of Age* (1996, original *La Vieillesse* 1970). It is an extensive work that brings together scientific, anthropological, and historical research on the phase in life generally called 'old age'. Old age is a category that the World Health Organisation (WHO) currently defines as follows:

The age of 60 or 65, roughly equivalent to retirement ages in most developed countries, is said to be the beginning of old age. In many parts of the developing world, chronological time has little or no importance in the meaning of old age. Other socially constructed meanings of age are more significant such as the roles assigned to older people; in some cases it is the loss of roles accompanying physical decline which is significant in defining old age. Thus, in contrast to the chronological milestones which mark life stages in the developed world, old age in many developing countries is seen to begin at the point when active contribution is no longer possible. (Mark Gorman cited by WHO 2014: unpaginated)

This definition reflects the social and cultural dimension of age(ing) laid out earlier in this chapter in reference to the works of Woodward. Beauvoir's work on old age, correspondingly, discusses the meaning of it across time and different social systems. Beauvoir states that "old age can only be understood as a whole: it is not solely a biological but also a cultural fact" (1996: 13). She critiques the generalisation of the aged as a category and points to the naturalisation of the devalued role of the aged, as well as their oppression and marginalisation in capitalist societies. Her examination details the ways in which markers of old age come much earlier for the poorer classes and how changes in the social roles of the aged can be historically traced. For this she holds society accountable:

> But although old age, considered as a biological fate, is a reality that goes beyond history, it is nevertheless true that this fate is experienced in a way that varies according to the social context: and conversely, the meaning or the lack of meaning that old age takes on in any given society puts that whole society to the test, since it is this that reveals the meaning or the lack of meaning of the entirety of the life leading to that old age. (Beauvoir 1996: 10)

About the actual society in which she lived, she writes: "As far as old people are concerned this society is not only guilty but downright criminal. Sheltering behind the myth of expansion and affluence, it treats the old as outcasts" (Beauvoir 1996: 2). These quotes show that although Beauvoir's work concentrates on a specific age group, the philosophical and socio-political questions she raises concern all ages.[3]

In contrast, the second seminal text on the subject, *The Double Standard of Aging* by Susan Sontag (1972), highlights the intersection of the cultural categories age and gender, and it traces the markers of a gendered age bias as early as the end of youth.

> Getting older is less profoundly wounding for a man, for in addition to the propaganda for youth that puts both men and women on the defensive as they age, there is a double standard about aging that denounces women with special severity. [...] The double standard about aging shows up most brutally in the conventions of sexual feeling, which presuppose a disparity between men and women that operates permanently to women's disadvantage. [...]

---

3 | *The Coming of Age* has been largely neglected in academic discourse about the philosophy of Beauvoir. However, more recently her specific contribution to the age(ing) discourse has entered into discussions. See for example Silvia Stoller (ed.), *Simone de Beauvoir's Philosophy of Age: Gender, Ethics, and Time* (2014).

> [F]or most women, aging means a humiliating process of gradual sexual disqualification. Since women are considered maximally eligible in early youth, after which their sexual value drops steadily, even young women feel themselves in a desperate race against the calendar. They are old as soon as they are no longer very young. (Sontag 1972: 31-32)

The discourses on the devaluation of old age and on the gender difference concerning the meaning and consequences of age(ing) have been developed in the field of age studies since these pioneering works of the 1970s. Scholars such as Schwaiger (2006), Turner (1994) and Mike Featherstone (1991) have all discussed the influence of a capitalist and consumerist society on our understanding of age(ing). Currently all theorists who analyse dominant views on age(ing) emphasise also its gender inequality, one in which women experience the marginalisation of older people earlier than men do and "face graver social and economic consequences" (Heather Addison 2010: 13).[4] As such this field of study identifies and attempts to overcome the blind spot feminism most often has had in regard to older women and "the fact that ageing has been virtually ignored as an issue important to women" (Woodward 1999: xi). In addition to Woodward (1991, 1999, 2002, 2006), scholars such as Schwaiger (2006, 2012) and E. Ann Kaplan (2010) have all made relevant contributions to the research on gendered age(ing). My research builds on their work as well as on my own experience as a female dancer. Therefore, if not always explicitly, this research, in particular the two performances *The Fountain of Youth* and *The Fountain of Age* take a 'gender reflective'[5] perspective on age(ing) and work against the wider cultural emphasis toward male, youth oriented cultures.

---

4 | In this article Addison interestingly examines the intersection of gender, age, and consumerist ideology in pre-war Hollywood film productions.
5 | My use of the term gender reflective is informed by and a translation of the German term 'geschlechterreflektiert' employed by political theorist Katharina Debus, gender theorist Andreas Hechler, and sociologist Olaf Stuve (e.g. 2012, 2015).

Moreover, I define age studies as a cross-disciplinary field. This means I refer to age studies as a field of critical inquiry in which scholars from a diversity of disciplinary backgrounds investigate age. They use a wide range of methodologies to enter an international and interdisciplinary theory debate on age, its cultural images, social challenges, philosophical implications and practices of 'doing age' (Haller 2010b).[6] What separates age studies from the field of gerontology is that the research interest is not limited to old age. Age studies researchers react to the impossibility to clearly define when 'older' or 'old' begins (the quote from WHO above shows that this is widely acknowledged). They also react to the analysis that age related normative attributions and devaluation mechanisms could take effect much earlier in life than around statutory retirement age. Sontag's discussion of women being "old as soon as they are no longer very young" (1972: 32) underscores this notion.

Hence, the focus of age studies is to deconstruct the naturalisation of the (gendered) life course and to overcome the separation of age cohorts, which are never innocent and purely descriptive, but normative and defined by their respective discriminatory attributions. Mechanisms of separation in general are extensively discussed by Foucault (e.g. 1995, 2003), who offers a substantial analysis of how subjectivity in modernity gets constituted through dividing discourses of sanity and insanity, productivity and the unproductive, normality and delinquency. He traces how individuals lose their subject status by procedures of medicalisation, pathologisation, or deviation. Being acknowledged as subject, however, is central for retaining one's agency, which is why the separation of age cohorts in modern Western societies needs to be critically questioned and reviewed. Of late, questions of agency are therefore raised not only in relation to old age but as well in relation to the 'institutionalisation

---

6 | 'Doing age' is a term, used by age theorist Haller and others. The term emphasises the performativity of age and is as such a translation or application of the term 'doing gender' as used for example by Judith Butler, originally coined by Candace West and Don H. Zimmerman (1987).

of childhood', and the separation of children from adults, labelled 'youth moratorium', has been critically discussed (Wouter Vandenhole ed.al. 2015: 3-4).

The main focus of my research, however, is not the entire spectrum of age but narrowed down to adult practicing dancers and the experienced threat of physical decline and cultural stigmatisation starting with midlife or even earlier. Gullette makes this threat transparent in her book *Aged by Culture* (2004). In it she radically critiques the generally unquestioned pairing of age(ing) with the notion of decline, decay, and loss as an authoritative "decline-narrative" serving a "flawed and injurious [age-] ideology" (2004: 13). According to Gullette the 'grand narrative' (Jean-Francois Lyotard 1984) of a natural life course in contemporary Western culture is a progression throughout youth with a peak at early midlife. She argues that this peak is generally perceived to be reached at an increasingly younger age, followed by an accordingly extended decline. To suspend this grand narrative Gullette proposes to redefine "aging [...] as constitutive aspect of all identities, and identities [as] an achievement of aging" (2004: 138). She encourages, for example, a personal reconsideration and retelling of ones age autobiography (Gullette 2004: 141) to transform age consciousness and create new, positive age narratives (see my age autobiography above).

While I agree with the need to critique such a stereotypical grand narrative of a life course, I see the strategic encouragement of positive age narratives furthered in *Aged by Culture* as well as *Agewise* (Gullette 2011) as problematic. I argue that Gullette's activist agenda, whilst politically valuable and at times necessary, tends to simply replace negative stereotypes with positive ones. If the dominant concept of the decline narrative, as identified by Gullette and others, is recognised plainly as needing to be challenged and replaced, the alternative, a no less stereotypical positive narrative of progress, growth and seniority, in turn smothers the articulation of any negative notions connected to the process of age(ing), and keeps the discourse inside an unhelpful dualistic logic.

In fact, Woodward makes clear this danger of substituting negative stereotypes on age(ing) with seemingly positive ones in *Against Wisdom: The Social Politics of Anger and Aging* (2002). In it she deconstructs "old age wisdom" as one of the most popular counter-narratives to age(ing) as decline and interestingly places the pairing of old age and wisdom into the larger context of "the social politics of emotions as they relate to life stages" (2002: 187). She critiques the wisdom of age as a topos that serves as just another "screen for ageism" (2002: 187). According to Woodward, achieving wisdom, which supposedly comes with age, brings along with it poise and philosophic calm in its male connotation, serenity and tranquillity in its female version. She writes: "With its emphasis on detachment, wisdom justifies the disengagement theory of aging, the theory that older people "naturally" withdraw from their social roles so as to make their ultimate disappearance – death – less difficult for the smooth functioning of society" (Woodward 2002: 206). Woodward claims that the ideal of wisdom prohibits emotions and the related politically activating energy of anger and rage necessary to fight ageism. This is an important point she makes here. However, as will become clear in the following chapters, "a rhetoric of anger – as a strategy, calling up the cultural memory of militant women in the 1960s and evoking anger as a powerful binding force"(Woodward 2002: 187) is not a strategy that is often used in the practices or performances of dancers discussed in this research. Only the solo artist Wendy Houstoun, discussed in Chapter IV, uses, at times, a rhetoric of anger in her performance works.

The argument that superficially positive cultural images of age(ing) can actually limit the range of expression and participation of those idealised is also articulated in regard to representations of age(ing) in intergenerational dance works. As dance scholar Jessica Berson, who specialises in intergenerational dance, has written when discussing the work of choreographer Liz Lerman:

[The] erasure of the particular is an unintended effect that subverts Lerman's artistic and political goals. The older dancers in Lerman's choreography

> sometimes [...] have their edges worn away, smoothed out into a generalized vision of old age as wise, triumphant, and poignant. [...] While Lerman's teaching and choreographic processes empower seniors to create movement and find new modes of self-expression, the product of her concert work can generate stereotypical images and reaffirm dominant notions of old age. (Berson 2010: 178)

Berson describes here an approach in dance that, though meant to be anti-ageist, potentially takes part in (re)establishing culturally normative representations of people's behaviour, relationships and social roles, which repeat stereotypical age(ing) narratives and thereby confirm the simplistic dichotomy of youth and age.

The Ambiguity of Age(ing)

Schwaiger and Haller discuss an interesting strategy to undermine stereotypical and dichotomist conceptions of age(ing). They both underscore the notion of ambiguity as a feature of age(ing), but also as a subversive deconstructive strategy regarding the youth/age, progress/decline binary. Hence they lead the way towards stepping outside the confines of arguing the right or wrong of decline, progress, wisdom, seniority, anger, or triumph. For example, Haller points out that it is impossible to completely avoid thinking in binary terms. Nevertheless, she sees a possibility to subvert hierarchic binaries by way of endlessly postponing the decision between the two poles (Haller 2011: 361). In her article *Dekonstruktion der Ambivalenz* she draws on Derrida's concept of différance and Butler's concept of performativity to argue that ambiguity creates multiplicity on the level of meanings (Bedeutungsebene), which in turn can lead to productive ambivalences and irritations on the level of value judgements (Werteebene) (2011: 363). In the article *Ambivalente Subjektivationen* she further applies this to the field of gerontology. She argues that the emphasis on ambiguity and ambivalence destabilises bipolar discourses like those of productive and unproductive old age, autonomous and care needing old age, and makes it possible to reveal and critique their powerful effects on the individual as well as on society as a whole (Haller 2013: 26).

Schwaiger's arguments around the ambiguity of age(ing) connect to *Dancing Age(ing)* and questions of performing dance as public narratives and images on age(ing) even more clearly. In *To Be Forever Young?* (2006: 23-31), Schwaiger uses theorists Patricia Mellencamp and Rosalyn Diprose to argue that ageing, just like being female, is marked by ambiguity in relation to bodily boundaries and, as such, is potentially threatening to the ideal of bodily control, unity and stability. Building as well on Butler's theory of performativity, she suggests that the ambiguous performance of age, just as that of gender, is useful in undermining ageist cultural norms. Schwaiger proposes that such ambiguous age performance can "gradually lead to a change in the cultural perceptions and valorization of older body-subjects" (2006: 31).

However, gender theory has shown that a deconstructive approach to identity, in this case an ambiguous performance of age, also places the individual in a vulnerable position. In *Masculinities* (1995), sociologist Raewyn Connell explains the disorientation of trying to live one's male gender differently by using the term 'gender vertigo': "To undo masculinity is to court a loss of personality structure that might be quite terrifying: a kind of gender vertigo" (1995: 137). Vertigo thus points to the departure from the familiar path of gender or of age conventions as a risky endeavour that might dissolve not only practised social relationships but also one's definition of personhood.

Following these discussions on ambiguity and vertigo, I suggest that dance and theatre offer a space to safely explore the ambiguous performances of age(ing).[7] The culturally accepted frame of art allows

---

7 | Emilyn Claid in *Yes? No! Maybe...: Seductive Ambiguity in Dance* (2006) emphasises how ambiguity is a central issue in contemporary dance. Her work is not concerned with questions of age(ing). However, her detailed discussion of ambiguity from the performer perspective as well as from the audience perspective helpfully analyses how both sides

for playful, imaginative testing, and the sharing of more complex and more vulnerable ways of doing age(ing), without having to pass for a younger age or perform the ideal of old age as wisdom. Theatre can be a site to question and widen our ideas on age, age appropriate behaviour, and appropriate images of bodies of different ages. It can be a place to critically question our sense of 'tastefulness' regarding representations of age(ing). Appropriateness and taste as notions where aesthetic and social questions link is famously discussed in Bourdieu's seminal sociological study on taste. In *Distinction: A Social Critique of the Judgment of Taste* (1984) he shows the important link between aesthetic judgement and social difference. He analyses how taste is a fine-tuning of our place in society. Thus, tastefulness, in the performances of everyday life, as well as in the arts, on stage and in mass media, reflects our socio-cultural norms. Bourdieu shows that aesthetic judgement is strongly tied to one's social position, and that both are practised and inhabited through what he calls a 'sense of social orientation' embodied in one's habitus. He writes, "the habitus is necessity internalized and converted into a disposition that generates meaningful practices and meaning-giving perceptions" (Bourdieu 1984: 170). The dynamic shifting of taste in judging, for example music, dress or comportment, play a part in marking social distinction, they define and are defined by a "sense of one's place" (1984: 471) in the social world. Taste helps to determine where one 'feels at home', and where one feels displaced. It gives orientation on what is gender appropriate and what is age appropriate.[8] Taste is not fixed but sensitive to historical change and (sub)cultural conventions. In music, what might have started as avant-garde or underground might then become mainstream and finally elevator music. Similarly, a way of dancing, an attitude and dress code could be regarded as cool when performed by a young

---

can actively and consciously engage in multiple, contradictory doings, and oscillating meanings.

8 | I do not discuss the category of class here, which is central in Bourdieu's work but not the focus of this book.

pop star or in a specific cultural context, whereas it could evoke embarrassment and ridicule when the performer has passed youthfulness, when the fashion has changed, or the context is different. Accordingly, age related tastefulness, or a sense of age appropriateness is defined by age norms and therefore worth being highlighted and questioned.

Consequently, my performance practice *Performing Age(ing)* concentrates on an ambiguous performance of age as strategy to weaken the normative and gendered 'social orientation' of appearing as young as possible and/or replacing lost youthfulness with dignified behaviour and an appearance of seniority. Chapter IV will return to the discussion of ambiguity in regard to *Performing Age(ing)*. Corresponding to this, the video documentation of the two solo pieces and of the practical research process reveals how ambiguity manifests aesthetically in my artistic practice.

INTERSECTIONS OF AGE STUDIES AND DANCE STUDIES

Investigations into the cultural aspects of age(ing) from a scholarly perspective in the context of dance are relatively limited. Besides Schwaiger's work, extensive academic research projects have been carried out by only a few scholars, such as Sara Houston in the field of community dance (2005a, 2005b, 2005c, 2011), Helen Thomas, who researches social dance forms (2002, 2013), and Wainwright and Turner, who address the world of classical ballet (2005, 2006a, 2006b). But it is Schwaiger's work that explicitly draws on age studies in her discussion of professional Western dance, and it is her work that is of specific relevance for my own research in the field of contemporary dance. In *Ageing, Gender, Embodiment and Dance* (2012), Schwaiger traces the representational disappearance of dancers beyond their mid-thirties and positions such experiences in a general climate of ageism within Western culture. Her study is placed in the context of Australian contemporary dance and helpfully demonstrates how the naturalisation of a dancer's short career is fed by and feeds back into what Gullette theorises as the culturally induced decline narrative.

The term naturalisation is useful here as it points to the ways in which the early end of a dance career is left unquestioned and is understood in limited terms such as natural physical peak or early impairment due to the specific physical stress, hence reasons that are related to the construction of biological or functional age. In contrast to this view, a 2008 survey in Germany has shown that less than twenty percent of dancers brought their career to an end due to injury related reasons (Dümcke 2008: 23). The already mentioned international survey from 2004 states that "29 per cent of surveyed former dancers in Australia, 33 per cent of former dancers in Switzerland, and 35 per cent of former dancers in the U.S. reported that the health effects of injuries caused them to stop dancing" (Baumol, Jeffri, Throsby 2004: 8). Schwaiger's study identifies a range of other factors that have discouraged dancers from either performing or from the dance field altogether. "Family commitments and prohibitive financial and funding considerations" (Schwaiger 2012: 53) turn out to be crucial issues in handling a profession that offers very limited financial security and career options. She writes: "Australian dancers felt that Western cultures undervalued them, and that this was reflected in their economic disadvantage" (2012: 57). This suggests that the ageist tendencies in the macrostructures of dance, identified for the hierarchic company system as well as for the independent dance field are additionally set in generally precarious working conditions (macrostructures are discussed in the introduction). Waning powers and injury as symptoms of natural or profession specific decline therefore do not hold as only reason for youth conventions in dance.

To support the concept of decline as a cultural narrative present in dance, it is useful to also briefly consider the work of Nanako Nakajima. Her research compares traditional Japanese dance with North American post modern dance and the community dance field in the USA and the UK (2011). She quotes Kabuki critic Tamotsu Watanabe as follows: "One does not attain the ultimate level of artwork until one practices every day and lives longer. That is different from the old people who live longer only to play croquet. Aging is one fundamental element in Japanese art, rather, I would say, aging is the ultimate purpose in Japanese art" (Watanabe cited in Nakajima 2011: 102). Nakajima continues:

[T]he old dancer symbolizes lifelong dance practice. Behind these aesthetics, there is mistrust in dance technique that transcends dancers' physical ability. The issue of aging justifies this physical and aesthetic unification of dance and the dancer in Japanese art. Many professional dancers in traditional Japanese dance, such as Toshinami Hanayagi and Yachiyo Inoue the Fourth, continue dancing in their eighties and become recognized as intangible national treasures. Aging is thus the ultimate status of dancing for those professional dancers, and the audience wants to spend money to watch their dancing. (Nakajima 2011: 103)

Clearly, traditional Japanese dance does not follow a cultural narrative of peak and decline. Instead it employs concepts of technique, virtuosity, and professionalism in dance that are not bound to youth but rather to old age. In the light of this Japanese age-culture, Gullette's indictment of the negative cultural narrative of ageing in Western culture as ageist or more precisely as 'middle-ageist' (2004: 26) becomes more explicit. Traditional Japanese dance relies neither on renewing itself through a repetitious replacing of older dancers by younger dancers as done in most Western dance companies, nor is it in need for young performance works that represent fresh 'potential and raw talent in its promising beginnings'.

The discussions thus far on the construction of age(ing) in dance lead to the question of what alternative concepts on age contemporary improvisation-based dance might offer and, moreover, what would support the idea of its age critical potential, a question I asked in the introduction of this book. Schwaiger differentiates between visually codified, ballet oriented dance forms and experimental dance forms and locates the latter in the tradition of American postmodern dance from the 1960s and 1970s. She does not elaborate on the practices of what she calls experimental dance, but focuses instead on the concepts of embodiment and subjectivity rather than on the details of dance practice. Nevertheless, Schwaiger relates experimental dance to practices such as contact improvisation (2012: 65), release techniques, Body Mind Centering (2012: 68) and to dance artists such as Anna Halprin (2012: 144). Thus her reference points are similar to mine in my own improvisation-based dance making.

Dance scholar and choreographer Emilyn Claid usefully offers a more detailed insight into the possible effects of such practices for dance artists. She discusses the abovementioned approaches together with dance improvisation, Alexander technique and Aikido as "body-mind techniques", which took root in the UK in the 1970s (2006: 83-84). Claid analyses how the X6 collective[9] in that time used these practices to develop themselves as strong and independent artists, able and in power to redefine their roles as dancers, choreographers, and political artists outside the narrow conventions of modern dance and ballet:

X6 artists practiced body-mind techniques to un-fix the coded methods of training and allow our bodies a much wider range of movement possibilities for performance. We used them as pre-performance preparations for the body, as process not product, through which we could discover our individual movement vocabulary for performance. (Claid 2006: 80)

Although Claid's description does not actually refer to an age discourse, it can be read as confirming and giving practical detail to Schwaiger's discussion of experimental (or body-mind) practices. Indeed, Schwaiger argues that the further dancers remove themselves from codified forms such as ballet, and concern themselves with experimental and explorative approaches to the moving body

---

9 | X6 dance space, experimental dance studio and performance space 1976-1980, was run by a collective that included Claid, Maedée Duprès, Fergus Early, Jacky Lansley, and Mary Prestige.

and to performance, the easier it is to find a subjectivity beyond a narrative of decline. In *Performing One's Age* she explains:

> [B]ecause experimental approaches to movement or body practices are more attuned to individual bodies and their ways of moving than are ballet-based forms with their highly coded vocabularies, bodily signs of aging in the former lose their status as markers of which bodies can legitimately dance, and which can't. (Schwaiger 2005: 116)

Schwaiger and Claid's differentiation between codified and experimental techniques (to stay with Schwaiger's term) is partially supported by Wainwright and Turner's Bourdieu-based ethnographic study on embodiment in classical ballet. Their research shows that in the specific social context of classical ballet a performer's career is "invariably over by early middle age" (Wainwright and Turner 2006: 245). The career peak in this field has shifted from a dancer's late twenties to her early twenties and, as a result, "young dancers invariably feel much older than they look" (2006: 246).[10] Hence, to use again the X6 dancers as an example of dancers' pathways in experimental dance forms, these artists began their exploration of new ways of practicing movement and choreography at a chronological age when, in ballet terms, they were already too old, and when in fact they all already had ended their careers in ballet (compare Claid, 2006, but also the interviews with the editors of *The Wise Body*, Lansley [2011: 103-115] and Early [2011: 173-184]).

My appeal for the age critical potential of improvisation as an experimental practice is further supported by the work of dance scholars like Albright and Ross. At the conference *The Aging Body in Dance: Seeking Aesthetics and Politics of the Body through the Comparison of Euro-American and Japanese Cultures* (Berlin 2012) they opened up some possible theoretical routes for rethinking age(ing) in Western dance. For example, the less youth dependent ability of

---

10 | This resonates with the description of my psychological age in the age-autobiography at the beginning of this chapter.

giving into and using gravity in both the release-based approach to dance technique and contact improvisation was theorised by Albright as a metaphor for a counter-culture to the old American ideologies of 'upward mobility' and forced interventions. In light of the ongoing financial crisis and environmental damage, Albright argued that these old ideologies have reached their limits. She consequently called for intersubjective, non-combative and anti-ageist ways of acting in all spheres of life, implying that practices developed in dance, such as release-based work and contact improvisation, might serve as meaningful models (Albright in Martin 2012).[11]

Furthermore, Ross anticipated the advent of a new genre she termed 'end-of-life performances' (Ross in Martin 2012). This new genre could flourish if more dancers reject the convention of identifying dance with the physical qualities of youth and instead continue to create and perform dances into their old age. Her argument was informed by her research on Anna Halprin. Halprin, born in 1920, is a dancer with an exceptional performance career that reaches until today and who works extensively with improvisation.

Several participants at the conference discussed how dance might enable ways of dealing with and appreciating our bodily being beyond a focus on youth and used Butoh dancer Kazuo Ohno (1906 – 2010) as an example of this. Ohno is probably the most famous exception to mainstream youthfulness in dance and an impressive example of somebody dancing until his last breath. Significantly, Ohno, like Halprin, had worked through improvisation (see Mark Franko 2011, Nakajima 2011, Ohno and Ohno 2004, Ross 2007). On the whole, the conference pointed to a growing age discourse in dance studies, and much of the discussion supported my argument

---

11 | Gravity and the modulation of weight, as manifested in the dancing body, is investigated in the lineage of modern dance since the early twentieth century. Doris Humphrey in particular is known for developing a theory of 'fall and recovery' as the core principle of her movement style in the 1930s.

that improvisation is a practice within dance that can offer concepts of artistry beyond the narrow focus on youthful bodies.[12]

In line with the discourses prevalent at the conference, I argue that the positive attention given specifically to Ohno and Halprin is significant. While these two dancers currently serve as much discussed and highly regarded older performers of this century, some decades earlier this position was occupied by the iconic choreographers Ruth St. Denis and Martha Graham, who danced into their seventies. However, their continued presence on the stage in the 1960s was and continues to be received with much more ambivalence. St. Denis was derogatively labelled a "caricature of herself" (Shelton in Scolieri 2012: 103), and Graham a "self-parody" (Franko 2012: 176) and "embarrassing" (Rainer 2014: 3). The main criticism, however, is the attempt by these dancers to continue reproducing old images and past successes, which thus exposes St. Denis and Graham to mixed feelings that include both pity and ridicule. Nonetheless, it may be that St. Denis and Graham's radical insistence to perform into later life enabled the audiences and critics of dance in the 1960s to reflect on the relationship between dance and age(ing). They therefore may be seen to have a stake in the slowly changing public perception regarding old dancers, and to have paved the way for later generations and those old dancers celebrated today. Additionally, it could also be argued that Halprin and Ohno's dedication to the present moment in time, sensing and exploring the body in improvisation may have saved them from such negative evaluation.

There are other indicators of an age discourse emerging in the field. For example, the four-day international *Dance Congress*, the major discursive platform for dance in Germany held every three

---

12 | Other contributors at the conference were: Gabriele Brandstetter, Ramsay Burt, Jess Curtis, Susanne Foellmer, Mark Franko, Nanako Nakajima, Johannes Odenthal, Yoshito Ohno, Kikuko Toyama and Tamotsu Watanabe. See also the book *The Aging Body in Dance* that emanated from the conference (Nakajima and Brandstetter 2016).

years, named age(ing) one of its topics in 2013. I was invited as a speaker on this topic and therefore would entirely agree with dance scholar Katherine Mezur's conference report that states:

> There was a sense in every performance or presentation that the entire field of dance is just getting started on the possibilities and critical agency that lies in age studies. [...] We will come back to this again and again: How social change and aesthetic change, and a radical change in the dance world's view of bodies, techniques, and aesthetics need to radically evolve to catch up with the dancing across the spectrum of age. (Mezur 2013: unpaginated)

In positioning my own research in relation to the age(ing) discourses presented thus far I seek to support a notion of ongoingness in lieu of progress, peak, followed by decline. However, I do so without assenting a continuous growth narrative, such as is implied by Gullette and Nakajima. The problem in notions of growth, seniority, and also old-age wisdom is that they still create fixed attributions and a static hierarchy between different ages. They reiterate a sense of linearity and fixity of personhood and an ideal life course that can be gained or lost. Such dualistic concepts do not stand up to the complex and contradictory experiences, and to the diversity of actual age(ing) processes (an example being the age autobiography with which this chapter opened). They also do not bear up to the actual age diversity for example in the field of contemporary dance and to improvisation as a practice that allows dancers of any chronological age to search for ways to "enact a kind of embodiment that celebrates processes and emphasizes emergence and becoming" (Midgelow 2012: unpaginated).

However, when looking specifically at scholarly conceptualisations of dance improvisation it is striking that age(ing) is not an issue of explicit concern. I argue that it is not necessarily a conscious and active strategy of normalising the existing age diversity and appreciation for older practitioners in the field of improvisation, but rather result of the fact that older bodies simply do not contradict the questions and topics raised by improvisation and its scholarly discussions.

Improvisation Discourses

That improvisation discourses do not speak of age(ing) does not mean they cannot be informative for understanding the special potential of improvisation for rethinking age(ing) in and through dance making. I suggest that it is the focus on procedures and processes of improvisational artistic making on the one hand (see Hans-Friedrich Bormann, Gabriele Brandstetter, Annemarie Matzke 2010, Buckwalter 2010, Kent De Spain 2014, Lampert 2007), and the focus on questions of subjectivity on the other hand (see Albright 2003a, 2003b, Danielle Goldman 2010, Edgar Landgraf 2011, Midgelow 2012) which lead the way to improvisation's specific relationship to age(ing). Both topics are inherently connected because it is the central feature of improvised dance that the roles of choreographer and performer always coincide, as do process and product, maker and what is made, practicing dance and practicing the self (Albright and David Gere 2003, Agnes Benoit-Nader 1997, Bormann, Brandstetter, Matzke 2010, Buckwalter 2010, Erni Kask 2012).

The writings of practitioners, of theorists, or of theorising practitioners that focus on the processes and procedures of improvisation expose that the success, value or satisfaction of a singular performance, a specific physical capacity, or theatrical image are of far less importance then the processes of developing, employing, and eventually making visible the "strategies" (Lisa Nelson in De Spain 2014: 39), "tools", or "resources" (De Spain 2014: 35) of improvising, and the "learning what is becoming in the process" (Buckwalter 2010: 4). That the situation and the body changes, and that it is impossible to hold on to what was, however perfect or satisfying, neither contradicts nor exalts improvisation. Instead these are the basic assumptions from which to work. In other words, improvisation does not build on a concept of progress-peak-decline, but foregrounds open-ended processes of and for creative play and creative interaction within constantly changing possibilities and constraints. Hamilton, when interviewed for this research, articulates this point more graphically:

> You use what you've got. And if you are young and bouncy, fresh and beautiful, you use that. And if you get slightly senile you use it, unless you are dumb. There is always an active, creative element of the state you are in, whether that's super calm and highly enlightened or a little bit dizzy, lost and sliding in time, erratic, very precise – you use what you got. And those things change during time. But I don't see them like that you start with a whole bundle of things and then it just diminishes, or they just decay. I just don't see that. (Hamilton 2011, clip 18.2, min 2:50)

Hamilton, importantly, does not fix specific attributes to specific ages. The possible qualities are not seen as unfolding in a linear or inevitable manner, and he does not attach different value judgements to them. As a result, one could read it as the improviser showing interest in the always changing qualities, intensities, potentials, and difficulties that arise during a potentially lifelong journey of searching, finding, relating, and reacting to one's artistic material. One's own constantly changing body is one of these many materials. What is accumulated through such a process focussed improvisation practice over time is neither a repertoire of choreographies nor a catalogue of obligatory movement skills and patterns but rather strategies of discriminating between possibilities, procedures for embodied enquiry, and knowledge on possible ways "to become more present, in more multifaceted ways" (Midgelow 2013). In this sense improvisation is a self-practice, which means it is inseparable from the body and takes part in forming one's subjectivity.

As already mentioned in the Introduction there is not one fixed understanding of subjectivity. I use this particular term to highlight the movement and move-ability with which individuals make sense of their situated and relational lives in changing ways, and how practitioners of improvisation in particular perceive themselves as being unstable or "learning what is becoming in the process" (Buckwalter

2010: 4). Several theorists of improvisation connect improvisation practice with questions of subjectivity as the philosophical quest for understanding human agency and its limits. They all build on discourses that deconstruct the idea of a set and pre-given selfhood and describe improvisation as a practice to negotiate and possibly widen the individual's range of possibilities to act as a socially situated subject with a certain degree of agency.

The conceptualisation of improvisation proposed by Midgelow draws on contemporary feminist philosopher Rosi Braidotti's concept of the nomadic self, a concept which "explore[s] and legitimate[s] political agency, while taking as historical evidence the decline of metaphysically fixed, steady identities" (Braidotti 1994: 5). Midgelow theorises an improvisation practitioner, with Braidotti, to be nomadic, in other words to be "the kind of subject who has relinquished all idea, desire, or nostalgia for fixity. This figuration [the nomadic subject] [...] expresses the desire for an identity made of transitions, successive shifts, and coordinated changes" (Braidotti cited in Midgelow 2012: unpaginated).

Albright draws on phenomenology as developed by the philosophers Edmund Husserl, Martin Heidegger, and Maurice Merleau-Ponty. She summarises: "Generally speaking, phenomenology is the study of how the world is perceived, rather than the study of the essence of things as objects or images of our consciousness" (2011: 8). However, her phenomenological perspective is also informed by "feminist philosophers such as Simone de Beauvoir, Iris Marion Young, Elizabeth Grosz, and Judith Butler [who] have critiqued the universalist approach of this early phenomenology, stretching that philosophical discourse to include a consideration of cultural differences, all the while conserving the original focus on the corporeal as a key element in the constitution of subjectivity" (Albright 2011: 8). Albright argues that improvisation is "one of the few experiences that cultivates a self open to possibility" and a practice of "opening one's physical and psychic being to the unknown" (2003a: 257). Goldman calls improvisation "live, urgent, playful, intelligent, spontaneous interactions with constraint" (2010: 54) and links her discussion explicitly to Foucault's analysis of how the modern subject is subjected to power relations but also asserts itself in these relations which are "mobile, reversible, and unstable" (Foucault cited in Goldman 2010: 143).

A last example of how scholars of improvisation draw on deconstructive subject theories is Landgraf's *Improvisation as Art* (2011). Similar to Goldman, Landgraf defines improvisation in the following way: "rather than being the expression of unbridled freedom, improvisation must be seen as a mode of engaging existing structures and constraints" (2011: 11). Without understanding the subject as completely autonomous, and equipped with an inherent and presupposed freedom, the improvising self has agency, but "as result, not as source of a continued, improvised practice" (2011: 18). Landgraf draws on Butler's concept of performativity, which analyses gender identity to be constructed through repetitious performative acts or doing. He highlights that Butler explains this as being "a practice of improvisation" (Butler 2004: 1). This act of practicing one's gender improvisationally evolves just as an artistic improvisation "as a simultaneous reiteration and alteration process" in which the individual engages while staying always in relation and in response to the social world, its norms and constraints (Landgraf 2011: 17). Hence each theorist in a different way emphasises the interpenetrative movement between improvisation practice and a subjectivity understood to be unstable, situated, relational and in process.

I suggest that these discussions of improvisation and subjectivity offer a more abstract and philosophical entrance to understand the very specific relationship between improvisation practice and age(ing). However, they can be seen to come to a similar point than the already mentioned practice-tool oriented discussions of improvisation. Both branches of improvisation discourse highlight that in improvisation dance is practiced without the goal of a final form and ending point. In the same way, the self is practiced and accepted as never ultimately defined nor undefined, never completely full nor devoid of possibility, but at any point of life in the process of change and becoming. Thus the following chapter focuses on how the practitioners of improvisation who participated in this research conceptualise their art making and their age(ing) process. It, thereby, tries to disclose what I call the implicit age critique of improvisational dance practice.

Summary

As the previous discussion demonstrates, my research shares a similar set of concerns found in age studies to reconfigure and challenge dominant understandings of age(ing). It does so by revealing the cultural construction of the term age, by unravelling some of its underlying concepts and categories, and by accentuating some of its normative narratives. Throughout the first part of the chapter I seek to present age as a complex and often contradictory mix of categories and epistemologies, exploring the core questions under examination in age studies, and addressing in more detail cultural age narratives like the progress-peak-decline narrative or the old-age-wisdom narrative. These discussions show how age studies, an area concerned with the ageist distinctions and stereotypes deeply ingrained in our culture, can give rise to a revision of widely accepted conceptions of age(ing). Moreover, I introduce the notion of ambiguity as a potential strategy to undermine the repetition of ageist stereotyping and age norms communicated through notions of age appropriateness or age related tastefulness. The second part focuses upon current age discourses in dance. In doing so, it demonstrates how the assumed youthfulness of dance and the naturalisation of dancers' short careers, institutionalised in the macrostructures of professional dance, mirror and support the grand narrative of decline. Furthermore the chapter starts a discussion on the role of improvisation practices and practitioners in the current discursive shift in dance towards a growing acceptance, interest, and valuation of age(ing) bodies in dance. Finally, it conceptualises improvisation as an artistic practice that favours process and ongoingness over product or form, and that is linked to a subjectivity unstable, situated, relational, and in process. By doing so it lays the ground for the discussion of the implicit age critique of improvisation practice in the following chapter.

III. Improvising Age(ing)

Introduction

This chapter deals with improvisation as a practice, one that foregrounds open-ended processes of and for creative play and creative interaction within constantly changing possibilities and constraints. Building on my age theoretical discussion in both the Introduction and Chapter II, it develops the proposal that specific aspects of improvisational practice are implicitly age critical. This means they take part in "undoing" age(ing) (Haller 2010b: 216) and in being less "governed" by detrimental age norms (Foucault 2007: 45), even if not always knowingly or purposefully. To argue for the implicit age critique in improvisation I first show how expert improvisers build what I call microstructures for sustained artistic practice in a youth oriented professional field. Second, I discuss how they deal with physical constraints. And third, I turn to how dialogical practice formats in improvisation foster reflexivity and discuss how the specific reflexivity practiced can be seen to offer practical tools for rethinking age(ing).

The chapter focuses on improvisation as it has been developed and practiced by Chung, Crisp, Eriksson, Hamilton, Morrish, and Simson, who were all asked to participate in this research, as well as on my own improvisation practice. The data used in this chapter is mainly comprised of the expert knowledge on improvisation and age(ing), which I have gathered in interviews, artistic responses and my engagement with *Solo Partnering*, my main artistic research practice during this inquiry. The data itself is made available in the online video collection. Each of the artists discussed works with a particular and individualised approach to improvisation. However, most draw on the principles and the practice of contact improvisation as one of their main sources or influences. Therefore this chapter also discusses specific aspects of contact improvisation that have particular relevance to the discourse of age(ing).

Building Microstructures for Sustained Artistic Practice

As discussed at the end of Chapter II, improvisation is invested in exploring an ever changing, always age(ing), embodied self that is not fixed to notions of a physical and/or artistic peak. The process orientation of improvisation resists the idea of an ultimate realisation of one's artistry, either in youth, as in ballet, or in old age, as in traditional Japanese dance. However, the way dance artists relate to age(ing) depends not only on the practices they favour. As laid out in the Introduction, the youth oriented macrostructures through which artistic work is organised and realised in the professional field of dance also have a stake in how artists perceive and relate to age(ing), given that these structures determine the possibility to gain economic and cultural viability or even valorisation. To develop this point further I turn to examine specific activities and approaches developed and cultivated by the participating improvisers that serve as microstructures for sustained artistic practice. While many of these structure-building activities are not exclusive to improvisation, I regard them to be fundamentally characteristic for this form of dance practice

Operating at a Distance from the Macrostructures of Dance

It is significant that all improvisers discussed in this chapter are all keenly aware of being artists who create their own particularised artistic work. They all developed and keep fostering their artistic work as independent and freelancing creative/creating artists, defining their own artistic path, and art making. Hamilton for example stresses:

I made decisions in my mid-twenties to be autonomous, therefore, to be busy with primarily my own work from then. That means that you view your body in realistic terms to that moment. And that means that your relationship to the ageing process is very different. Because you are not based against somebody else's scale, that you gain and then diminish from. You are always in parallel with your own development, changing, ageing right from early on. (Hamilton 2011, clip 18.1, min 9:35)

As individually and independently working artists they all operate at a distance from the established macrostructures in dance, not only regarding hierarchically organised institutions, but also regarding the competitive dynamic of repeatedly attracting the attention of the mediators and funding bodies in the project based independent dance field. None of them exclusively concentrates on realising funded performance projects. Instead, they all attempt to gain a degree of economic independence from the current project funding system. To make this possible they all follow a mixed mode strategy of artistic and economic survival in which teaching improvisation plays a major role. Furthermore, all pursue non-consumerist lifestyles. Hamilton articulates it in this way:

I know that for myself and five, six other people, they made very particular strategies of how to survive. All of the ones I'm thinking of now were based on how to live low rent and that involved for instance living in the countryside, growing your own food. [...] These are really deliberate and concrete decisions. That has enabled those people to have the time, space, money to keep in attendance with their own body and their own making. [...] There are lots of different ways within that, but the essential thing being a situation that they can weather, which allows them enough space to keep playing. [...] In all the people that I know there is really a concerted and defined effort [...] to do that. (Hamilton 2011, clip 18.1, min 17:10)

The strategies and possibilities to maintain a degree of economic independence are individual and diverse. Nevertheless, what the interviewed artists share is that they do not participate extensively in the competition for projects, residencies, festivals, production networks, but rather explore mixed modes of financing their art making. This is practical, not least because of the focus on youth in funding circles and curating structures (discussed in the Introduction). Additionally, writers such as Kunst suggest that even for older dancers who are successful in the bid for funding and visibility, this mode of artistic production is not necessarily artistically satisfying since the individuals experience time deprivation and deadline pressure.

> [C]ontemporary modes of working suffer from a real deprivation of time – an actual one, not only a theoretical one: we never actually *have time*. What we lack is the actual time of the present, because we have sold off the present in return for a project outline. [...] The goal is always to reach something within the horizon of the project. In that sense, the project becomes the ultimate horizon of our experience. (Kunst 2012a: unpaginated)

Kunst's analysis suggests that independent dancers find themselves in a situation that is the opposite of having the time to play and to keep in attendance with one's body, a situation that Hamilton in the quote above claims as vital for an artist. The difficulty of securing time for creative play and bodily research is confirmed by Crisp. She reports to have moved away from trying to succeed inside the dominant production and distribution structures, which she experiences as draining. "The career, the career, you really have to be out there, keep looking for these producers, pushing shit uphill, and convince them of your work – I can't be bothered any more. I'm "come to me". I just have too much joy in the work I'm doing, so I'm more led by joy than career ambition and need for recognition" (Crisp 2012, clip 20, min 23:50).

Part of such a position at the margins of the arts market is also the fluid definition of these improvisers' art making. In particular contact improvisation is a field in which artists actively blur the boundaries between performance, practice, and teaching – conceptually as well as practically. This blurriness makes distinctions between being 'performer' or 'choreographer' or 'teacher' increasingly irrelevant, and the possibly attached hierarchic order, which is so defining, for example, for the company structure is undermined. The interviews with Simson and Chung confirm this attitude. Chung states:

At some point I felt like I grew less interested to perform, because I wasn't quite sure why I was doing it other than because people asked me to. So I go in and out of it. Teaching is more constant – for a number of reasons. There is the financial, also the creative [...]. I learn more from the teaching process than from the performing process. (Chung 2011, 19.1, min 26:30)

Chung's statement helps to comprehend this blurred understanding of an artist's practice as it articulates how teaching improvisation is more than just a strategy for economic survival. Instead it is one of several modes of his long-term artistic research. Furthermore, Crisp's suggestion above that she has "too much joy in the work" (2012, clip 20, min 23:50) hints at the fact that she, like other improvisers, regularly engages in in a wide range of different practice and performance formats. Not all of them are visible or sellable as artistic 'products' and therefore difficult to attract producers. However they all constitute her artistic work. She teaches workshops, and performs in informal situations that are often connected to her workshops, instead of solely focussing her time and energy on negotiating the established modes of current art production. In other words, she engages in building a microstructure to sustain her professional practice, which she describes as personally and artistically satisfying, despite the limited public recognition.[1]

---

1 | Since 2006 I saw her dance in a range of studio performances at different venues. Between 2006 and 2008, for example, Crisp curated the studio performance format *The Crocodiles* in Paris, in which I also performed. Likewise, in 2011 she was my guest in my series *Susi & Gabi's*

With this example in mind, operating at a distance from the macrostructures of dance improvisation can be regarded as a mode of practicing the improvising subject's 'relative' agency, as noted in my improvisation and subjectivity discussion in Chapter II. To paraphrase Landgraf, quoted in the last chapter, staying at the margin can be understood to be an improviser's mode of creatively and practically engaging existing ageist structures and constraints. It enables the continuity of a process oriented artistic practice in a project and youth oriented field. To return to Woodward's argument on including anger in the palette of emotions and driving forces of age(ing) subjects, I want to emphasise that this way of securing one's personal art making does not necessarily mean the absence of feelings such as anger, disappointment, or discontent with the established macrostructures of dance. However, in accordance with the basic principles of improvisation discussed earlier these artists decide to focus on actively affirming and nourishing what is possible rather then scandalising and fighting against the obstacles they encounter.[2]

Salon in Berlin. She performs when possible in big festivals, but does not consider that her main aim (any more). Similar ways of working and performing, exemplified here through Crisp, can be applied to all the improvisation-based performers interviewed for this research.

2 | Braidotti in particular discusses affirmation as a critical project. She passionately "affirm[s] the affirmative" (2006a). She positions her concept of nomadism in the wake of philosopher Gilles Deleuze as developing an ethics that "is essentially about transformation of negative into positive passions, that is, about moving beyond the pain. This does not mean denying the pain but rather activating it, working it through. Again, the positivity here is not supposed to indicate a facile optimism or a careless dismissal of human suffering. What is positive in the ethics of affirmation is the belief that negative affects can be transformed"(2006b: 247). She also distinguishes between what she calls the affirmative and the melancholic branch of poststructuralism. The former includes for example Deleuze, philosopher Felix Guattari and, as a next generation, herself. The

Engaging in Collaborative and Peer-Supportive Practice Formats

Another characteristic of how these artists create microstructures for a continued and potentially lifelong practice is through an engagement in explicitly collaborative and peer-supportive practice formats. With the term peer-supportive I refer to ways of working that emphasise inclusion and reciprocity. This suggests an alternative and an implicit critique of the "dividing practices" (Foucault 1982: 777) characteristic for the macrostructures of professional dance, such as the division between professional and amateur dancers, funded and unfunded productions, teachers and performers, or the division between young artists as supposedly new and innovative voices and older/nor more new artists suspected to be gridlocked.[3]

Eriksson, Chung, and I all see a regular engagement in contact improvisation jams as a central component of personal artistic research/practice. Since 1997, an integral part of my dance practice is to regularly attend at least one of the weekly contact improvisation jams in my hometown Berlin, Germany. Jamming means abandoning the role of performer or teacher, and participating in communal practice. It means learning with and from other contact dancers of all levels. The concept of the jam derives from the jam session culture of improvising jazz musicians. It is also inspired by martial arts training in which practitioners with different levels of experience train together.[4] As Chung explains: "[The jam] is my laboratory, that's why I love jamming, because it's a laboratory in itself, about

---

melancholics, by contrast, rather focus on loss, lack and mourning and include psychoanalyst Jacques Lacan, Derrida and, as Braidotti's contemporary, Butler (Braidotti in Martin 2014).

3 | Foucault discusses the division of subjects with focus on the categories "the sane and the mad, the sick and the healthy, the criminals and the good boys'" (1982: 778).

4 | For more detailed information on contact improvisation jams and contact improvisation in general see for example: *Sharing the Dance* by

what's working, what doesn't. What's new, what's interesting? Why am I bored, why am I not? What's happening? [...] It's a free association, free stream of consciousness kind of thinking, but physically" (Chung 2011, clip 19.2, min 16:55). Chung's foregrounding of his jamming practice again underlines the importance of having 'time to play', to reflect and to imagine other 'horizons', something advocated by Hamilton and lamented on by Kunst.

It is also worth noting that in my own dance practice contact improvisation jams are as well a site where I experience intergenerationality, and am confronted with varied processes of exclusion and inclusion of difference. In jams I have danced with people twenty, thirty or even forty years older than me and, now that I am in my mid-forties, also with people twenty years younger. From these experiences jams might be seen as contributing to normalising intergenerational social, physical, and artistic exchange in dance and put into practice the call in age studies to overcome the separation of age cohorts (as discussed in Chapter II).[5]

Additionally, Morrish stresses the importance of setting up low-maintenance peer-practice situations, which can support artists to continuously cultivate their individual performance research, improvisational skills, and artistic play outside the system of art project funding. According to him practicing is key to artistic sustainability. "In the shared practice, the real support of the shared practice is to keep doing it. So especially in my lifestyle, where I'm travelling a lot,

---

Novak, 1990, the journal *Contact Quarterly*, or *Contact Improvisation* by Cheryl Pallant, 2006.

5 | Lately there is also a growing interest in expanding the age range in jams also by including children into the practice. Besides family friendly jams there are currently classes in which parents learn to dance contact improvisation with their children. 2012 Improviser and choreographer Itav Yatuv started the education program ContaKids after a video of him jamming with his 2-year-old child became a 'youtube hit' (www.youtube.com/watch?v=zkreiRt8GEY) (personal conversation with the artist).

I share practice as much as I can, so I stay in the process" (Morrish 2014b, clip 16, min 9:35).

Similarly, I organise or participate in many informal and formal contexts, as outlined below, in which peer-practice situations are central. Besides jamming, my practice of *Solo Partnering*, drawing upon an approach developed by Morrish, is part of my own investment in microstructures for sustained practice (this practice is introduced in Chapter I and is further discussed later in this chapter). I also, at times, facilitate the teacher meetings that precede the annual *International Contact Improvisation Festival* in Freiburg, Germany.[6] Such engagements reflect my commitment to developing non-hierarchic peer-supportive activities. Furthermore, I regard the performance series *Susi & Gabi's Salon* (also addressed in Chapter I), conceived and conducted together with Reuter, as another example of a peer-support activity. The salons are a platform for exchange and shared reflection between invited artists, but also between these artists and the audience. They foster public visibility and public discussion on improvisers' practices and performance works.

To summarise what I have outlined above, I describe microstructures as choices and endeavours that seek to nourish a long-term and enriching artistic practice that is process oriented, dynamic and open to change. In Chapter II I cited Albright theorising improvisation as a practice of "opening one's physical and psychic being to the unknown" (2003a: 257). I suggest that this take on improvisation characterises it as a self-practice that is neither bound to any specific age cohort, nor to completion. Building microstructures enables the continuity to which such open-ended practices aim. Thus it sidesteps the structural constraints posed by the focus on youth in the established macrostructures of hierarchically organised institutions or the market for independent performance projects. Such engagements assist the individual in continuing to dance and perform

---

6 | For more information on this major gathering of contact improvisation practitioners see: http://www.contactfestival.de/english/festival/festival.htm

beyond early midlife. This does not mean that the dancers engaged in this work necessarily have longevity, or are interested in an explicit critique of the age(ing) culture in dance, or that they have their own future consciously in mind when forming their particular pathways as improvisation-based artists. Moreover, these microstructures are not without problems, as they can produce their own micro-hierarchies and exclusions (see for example Novack's discussion of informal hierarchies in contact improvisation throughout Chapter Eight in *Sharing the Dance*, 1990).[7] Nonetheless, what I suggest here and what I call implicitly age critical is that improvisation-focussed dancers develop ways of evading established structural constraints and a structurally established ageism by creating modes of working that give them a sense of agency and open-ended process as well as an actual and continuing presence in the professional field.

I now clarify further how improvisation practices implicitly takes part in interfering with and critiquing the dominant age(ing) culture in dance. To further explicate the age critical potential of improvisation practice I shift the focus away from improvisers' strategies of negotiating structural constraints and deepen the analysis of improvisers' engagement with their own moving bodies by focussing on how they negotiate their shifting physical constraints.

DEALING WITH PHYSICAL CONSTRAINTS

Whilst in age study discourses physical constraints are not a key concern, in dance they are of crucial importance and are tied up with how we perceive ourselves as dancers. What I call again implicitly age critical and will specify in the following is how improvisation

---

7 | Novack analyses how in contact improvisation, when seen as a community of practitioners, egalitarian and inclusive values upheld in the practice can be contradicted by unequal distributions of power between participants that may arise from different skill levels, different social roles within the group, or diverging objectives of practice.

practice is open to integrate experiences of physical constraint and losses of athletic ability as part of its creative and investigative processes and procedures. In this way improvisation implicitly questions the notion of waning powers and injury as the reasons for a dancer's short career.

For dancers who improvise their art making is bound to their individual bodies, the distinction between maker and what is made dissolves, and practicing dance and practicing the self is inherently merged. Hamilton argues that this is not a weakness but rather a strength, because it leads improvisers, and all dancers who create and perform their own works, to stay tuned to their particular physicality.

So literally your relationship to your movements and where they come from and how to stretch and demand from them without abusing the body is hot-wired in the whole time. It's not simply that the same dance just continues to go on. It was engineered autonomously, and that gave it a kind of health in its effects on the body rather then a detrimental, abusive influence on the body. It's not just a case of continuing to dance later in your life. How you were dancing all the time is actually the issue. (Hamilton 2011, clip 18.1, min 10:14)

All artists quoted in this chapter cultivate what Hamilton here describes as a non-abusive, non-detrimental relationship to their bodies. The ways in which they develop such non-abusive, non-detrimental body practice are diverse and the influences or lineages present in each of these individual dance practices are manifold. Simson, for example, frequently references aikido and contact improvisation to have influenced her personal practice. Crisp refers to release techniques, Body-Mind Centering and contact improvisation. Chung, besides contact improvisation, works with knowledge from shiatsu and fascia research.[8] Again, this does not mean that these artists, or improvisers

---

8 | The term fascia describes the network of different connective tissues in the body. For more information see: https://fasciaresearchsociety.org/; http://www.fasciaresearch.de/

in general, do not struggle or experience anger or frustration in situations of physical impairment. However, my research suggests that such an emphasis on first person somatic informed research into the moving body, and on composing and relating to the reality of the 'here and now' in improvisation allows dancers to negotiate their individual physical constraints within and through dance practice.

Maintaining Practice

As part of this research, Chung explains how the jam can be used to clarify and ground his artistic curiosities. I support this idea, but go a step further and draw on my own experiences of dealing with physical constraints. This practice format provides me with a space to keep moving with my peers and to explore my potential to self-heal in periods when I have to deal with acute physical challenges or temporary disabilities. Due to the improvisational form and the somatic sensitivity cultivated between jam practitioners I have never found myself completely isolated and unable to dance with others. Similarly, the writings of Albright (see for example: 2003a: 257-265, 2003b: 210) stress contact improvisation's potential to deal with impairment, temporary, or permanent disability, but also to deal with fear and loss in general. The possibility to maintain my practice and be part of a community of practitioners, despite my shifting physical failings, allows me to work on overcoming my own oversimplified interpretations of my weaknesses and impairments, issues I might otherwise see as signifying the end of my performance career.

Simson too, reflects on the physical and mental challenge of injury and impairment and the connection to age(ing). The day before our interview she injured her back. While talking to the camera she deals with her back discomfort by resting on an Overball.[9] When asked how she will continue her artistic journey she says:

---

9 | An Overball is an inflatable soft ball of around 20 cm used in a range of training and rehabilitation methods such as Pilates. An Overball appears as well in my solo *The Fountain of Youth* (see clip 1).

Every time I have an injury I think: *oh God, is this it? Am I going to have to change my style?* But my body keeps, not recovering, but I feel like after so many years of this kind of study, there is some kind of honed intelligence, so that even when I have these things, it regenerates, and I go on. [...] So, I don't know where it's all going, but my plan is to continue. I cannot imagine not doing it. I'm sure as you get much older things shift, interests shift. But I don't know, I'm 55 and I'm still doing the same stuff. (Simson 2013, clip 15, min 13:30)

Central to Simson's statement are the ideas of 'honed intelligence' acquired and embodied through many years of study, as well as differentiating between recovering and regenerating. She senses that she cannot return to a body she once had/was, but as an experienced practitioner she keeps reforming and recreating it. Simson experiences and practices a body that is not static, and can also not return to (or 'recover') its previous state. Nevertheless, for Simson the body regenerates in intelligent ways and in that way continues to be a dancing body. She acknowledges that her body has limitations but experiences that long-term practice ('honing') can keep her individual limits dynamic. It is also illuminating to know that she did not hone, study, and deepen her improvisation throughout the years with the explicit objective to be able to dance into her fifties. Moreover, it has not been the goal of her improvisation practice to overcome physical constraints. Instead she *finds* herself continuing, regenerating, learning, still interested in her dance practice. This supports the idea that improvisation challenges the normative narrative of the youthful nature of dance, while not necessarily being based in an explicit longevity objective as for example traditional Japanese dances (see Chapter II).[10]

As noted by Simson, and in the description of my own experiences, there is an emphasis on the learning process as part of a continuing practice, which can help carry the dancer through times of injury.

---

10 | Simson speaks instead of a spiritual path she is on, which is by nature open-ended.

This learning process enables the avoidance of premature judgement – such as considering an injury to be the end a dancer's career. These learning processes are supported in improvisational dance practice since the experiential focus of the form allows for the continuity of physical exploration throughout a dancer's changing state of health or functional age. In turn, the experimental and somatically intelligent relationship to the body enables the actual recognition and refined awareness of constantly changing states of health or functional age in the first place. The emphasis on open-ended researching and responding to changing realities renders improvisation a practice of negotiating, balancing and integrating ambiguous states and multiple and shifting physiological challenges without leaning too heavily on oversimplified or static notions of healthiness and linear decline narratives.[11]

Paying Attention to Possibility

Accordingly, Chung, when asked how he imagines himself and his dancing to be in ten years time, states:

My hope is that I can still have the range and ability that I have now. But given that I might not be able to - within the range that I do will have then - that I can find an infinite world of possibilities within that. It's possible now, finding an infinite range of possibilities. The hope is, as a practised improviser, that that's possible in any situation. So I would think by then I would have that much more experience to realise that I can do that, or still continue to be there in no matter what situation, no matter what physical constraints may arise. It sounds idealistic, but that's the imagination. That's the beauty of improvisation. No matter what the situation is, it's

---

11 | With my age autobiography at the beginning of Chapter II I already proposed that age is an ambiguous mix of cultural constructions with contradictory meanings and definitions as well in regard to health and functional or biological age.

possible to create a number of things with it. That's why I find myself still doing it, still fascinated by it. (Chung 2011, clip 19.2, min 00:47)

Chung does not claim that improvisation conquers all the consequences of age(ing). However, he experiences his improvising as a way to find and trust new and artistically satisfying openings in any situation. Importantly, Chung does acknowledge the temporality of what he calls his range as dancer, performer, and artist. Although he anticipates potentially negative changes (e.g. physical limitations), they do not threaten his self-understanding as a dancer. That is because his artistry is not defined by a set of norms in terms of movement vocabulary or physical ability. More relevant to his dance practice is the principle of exploration, of continuously exploring pathways and procedures for open-ended searching and finding. Interestingly, Chung confirms these notions once again in the improvised trio with Eriksson and me in 2014 (clip 22). Despite the fact that in the time between our two meetings Chung has been injured, he is still in full agreement with his earlier statement.[12]

In the same vein, Morrish reflects on questions of temporary or permanent losses of physical capacity in this way:

I can remember when my ageing process first started. There were some very clear moments when I felt: *ah, I've turned a corner. Something has gone.* Often to do with going in and out of the floor in particular, which is often a joke I make when I perform. I could really feel this thing had gone and it would not come back. And the first time this happens to you, you are bit like: *ah, it's gone.* And then you start saying: *I've turned a corner.* And then

---

12 | Three years after the interview cited above, I met him again, together with Katarina Eriksson, whom I also interviewed in 2011. During this second meeting the three of us recorded a new, danced response to my quest for rethinking age(ing). This included the possibility to repeat, respond to, and eventually revise their statements from 2011. Chung stated that he had nothing to revise. My method of collecting expert knowledge by inviting artistic responses is discussed in Chapter I.

you realise, what a great new street. What an interesting new street I'm in. The one where I cannot do these things. But what can I do is actually what is relevant to me as an improviser. So as you get older the whole thing shifts. And if you are really engaged with improvisation then that happens unconsciously and automatically, because the job is to pay attention to where you are. So therefore now, my body doesn't choose to jump nearly as much as it did when it was thirty. (Morrish 2014b, clip 16, min 2:04)

Morrish seems particularly relaxed and emotionally calm regarding his functional losses over time. He stresses that finding new possibilities, new openings, and new interests within increasing constraints is inherent to an improviser's practice. According to this statement he is able to deal with loss because he works on staying fully engaged with the improvisational principle of focussing on the body, the situation, and the possibilities of the here and now. What is clear in his argument is that part of the work is to avoid lingering on options no longer available with a sense of mourning and melancholia.

Both artists' statements correspond to my more theoretical discussion of improvisation and subjectivity in Chapter II. In that chapter, I argued that an improviser practices a self "who has relinquished all idea, desire, or nostalgia for fixity" (Braidotti cited in Midgelow 2012: unpaginated). These artists' voices convey that this is not just a standpoint or an idea but rather a specific work to be done in and through an engaged and long-term artistic practice.

However, I argue that Morrish's resolved attitude towards functional losses is also a result of his practice not being driven by high impact dancing. He never saw himself or worked as a dancer in a conventional sense. Therefore it could be said that he has had less to lose: less of his performer-identity derives from the artistic and sensual satisfaction of fast, energised, virtuosic movements. Also the recognition received from others never relied on such qualities of dance, but rather on his ability to win over his audience with poetic and funny theatrical moments. Morrish always identified as an improviser whose work is based in the body (Morrish in Kask 2012: unpaginated), but not as a dancer with any of dance's particular movement and body ideals. In *Dancing Bodies* (1997) and *Dancing Bodies Ad Addendum* (2010) dance scholar Foster analyses a range of ideal dance bodies specific to particular dance genres and constructed in particular training regimes, such as the effort-hiding 'ballet body', the emotionally neutral and economic 'released body', or the grounded 'contact body' with reliable reflexes. Morrish's ambition as an improviser, in contrast, is not about any bodily quality but rather taking a biographical approach to performance. Or, in his words: "I go and pay attention to what is happening and do that fundamental, concrete work that keeps me present and keeps me representing who I am [...] the process is to keep finding out who I am" (Morrish 2014b, clip 16, min 10:05). That means the virtuosity he seeks is about finding ways of communicating and giving form to ideas, recognitions, or memories extracted from his biography. Emulating his body into movements or shapes for their own sake or in relation to any existing movement or body ideal is not a focus of his performance interest.

Whilst it is beyond the scope of this thesis to elaborate extensively on gender, it is worth noting a gender difference in the assertions presented thus far. While there are obvious practice-specific reasons for Morrish's resolved and relaxed attitude, it is striking that all male improvisers who participated in my study (Chung, Hamilton, Morrish) mirror his position. None of them expresses problems or fears concerning physical constraints in the present or for the future. In contrast, Simson, Eriksson, and I offer more ambivalent reflections on the experience of a changing body. Simson admits to moments of fear. Eriksson speaks of loss (discussed below). The discussion of my own practice, as well as my age autobiography and the video documentation of my practical research, all expose a certain effort to critically reflect on and deal with my assumptions of age, my expectations towards my dancing, and my experiences with a seldom fully, reliably available bodymind.[13] Therefore, my perspective

---

13 | See for example my dialogue with Crisp on weakness, stiffness, tiredness (clip 20, min 13:40) or my *Solo Partnering* improvisation *What I'm Good In Now* (clip 10).

underlines a self-reflexive work to be done, not a resolved relaxation about age(ing) and physical constraints brought solely about by practicing improvisation.

I argue that this difference in attitude confirms a basic observation of feminist scholarship. The men expose what Connell calls a 'hegemonic masculinity' (1995), which defines itself through qualities of the mind and their ability to manifest agency (Hamilton focuses on artistic autonomy, Chung on the ability to create, Morrish on the study of the self). Simson, Eriksson and I appear, in comparison, to identify more with the physical aspects of our being. We address in a more concrete way questions of the body, which partly corresponds to what is conventionally understood as femininity (Carol Gilligan 1982). We place emphasis on our vulnerability, while statements by Chung, Hamilton, and Morrish do not expose any obvious weakness or doubt. This brief look at deeply practiced and embodied gender roles is not meant to diminish the relevance of any of the statements discussed here, nor of the notion of improvisation as "one of the few experiences that cultivates a self open to possibility" and a practice of "opening one's physical and psychic being to the unknown" (Albright 2003a: 257, see my discussion of subjectivity in Chapter II). However, it shows that the range of possible relationships to the body and to the self we are able to recognise and realise is not infinite but, among other things, bound to how we perform our gender (Butler 1993). In other words, not all constructions of cultural and social differences are automatically dissolved or subverted in an implicitly age critical practice, but the intersection between age and gender that I discussed earlier with reference to Sontag (1972) continues to be formative for each of us.

Accepting Loss and Adjusting Focus

Returning to the core question of how to deal with physical constraints, a further aspect the interview with Eriksson discloses is that no form of improvisation practice leads to easy or permanent solutions concerning the physical vulnerability and the unpredictability of our bodily being. Experienced practice and self-study does not always provide the physical and mental tools for successfully negotiating one's individual physical changes and challenges. Eriksson explains that her compromised ability for having full-bodied, full-weighted and risk taking contact dances generated a crisis:

> It was in 1996 when my back at first got thrown out, and it has many times since then. [...] What was then and for many years after was the feeling: this is something temporary that I just have to figure out, and figure out what to do about it and then things are going to be great again. And then coming, as the years passed, to a realisation that ... Maybe five years ago I had almost a crisis around it. It was mostly around contact, not so much about performing at all, but it was almost a kind of grieving process: I'm not going to be the physical dancer that I see myself as, and want to be ... around contact, and how I use the body with other bodies. (Eriksson 2011, clip 17.1, min 15:00)

Eriksson describes the loss of a particular dance-body, one that can dare and enjoy what Albright analyses as a fundamental feature of contact improvisation, that is, "falling, being upside down, moving through fear and with a great deal of momentum, being out of control" (Albright 2003b: 260). Although Albright rightly proposes "somatic study and subtle bodily awarenesses" (2003a: 260) as another core feature of contact improvisation the aforementioned movement qualities and sensations do rely on a strong, able, and functionally young body. Such exhilarating moments of flying and falling are an important source of joy and fulfilment not only in contact improvisation but also in many other dance forms such as hip hop, street dance, martial arts forms such as capoeira or aikido, and many articulations of contemporary dance. Eriksson's statement reveals how this type of athletic joy is central to her as well and that she grieves this loss, irrespective of the fact that improvisation does not exclude dancers with less "fly-able" bodies. Subsequently, Eriksson found more narrative-driven forms of improvisation as a way to stay active as a dancer and performer, and continue to be acknowledged as a dancer.

But at the same time, there was this new interest in theatre or things that came up with the work with the improv group I was in, *Floke* [...]. It just came up, the characters and playing with words and sounds and things. So in my good moments, in that period, I thought, OK, so this is my opportunity to expand [into other areas of improvisation]. (Eriksson 2011, clip 17.1, min 16:26)

Although she continues to practice contact improvisation, it is the refocussing towards more theatre oriented improvisation that has allowed her to creatively negotiate her personal constraints.

I thus argue that improvisation, with its emphasis on developing investigative processes and procedures for artistic making, helps artists to shift their focal point without falling into ageist dichotomies. Eriksson, for example, does not describe a categorical change in her work from movement oriented to language oriented improvisation, but rather speaks of "expanding" her practice to language and character work. Nevertheless she acknowledges that this open-minded perspective is not developed or maintained without a struggle. Finally, she brings the narrative of her injury back to the subject of age(ing). When addressing the issue of coming to terms with a permanent physical restriction, she returns to the strategy shared by all improvisers discussed in this chapter, namely, to make whatever is available or present the material with which to work: "Ageing, I think, is the acceptance that this [the back injury] is not this temporary thing that is totally going away [...]. It is something I have to deal with and I have to carry with me. It's part of me. It's a wound. [*Smile*] It's material [to improvise with]" (Eriksson 2011, clip 17.1, min 18:40). [14]

---

14 | The complicity that Eriksson expresses in just saying "it's material" without any further explanation originates in our shared performance making history. Since 2008, Eriksson, Novak-Lindblad and I perform

In summary, I suggest that improvisers are involved in long-term processes of negotiating their shifting physical constraints with the "honed intelligence" (Simson 2013, clip 15, min 13:30) acquired and embodied through many years of study. It appears to be an integral part of improvisational practicing to work towards overcoming oversimplified interpretations of weaknesses and impairments, to shift, expand, and adjust one's individual physical and creative practice in accordance to a body that is understood not to be static but vulnerable and changing. Improvisers train themselves to focus on what is possible and available and to find an "infinitive world of possibility" (Chung 2011, clip 19.2, min 00:47) within the physical range and ability they have at a given moment. They do not take refuge in what Braidotti calls "facile optimism", but actively work towards what she calls "an affirmative project that stresses positivity and not mourning" (2006b: 237). I argue that by doing so they challenge and implicitly critique the normative narrative of the youthful nature of dance and a static concept of peak and decline.

PREPARING THE GROUND FOR RETHINKING AGE(ING)

To continue unearthing the potential of improvisation practice for rethinking age(ing) I now turn to dialogue and reflexivity. I propose that what is trained and developed in the often dialogical structures and principles of improvisation is reflexivity, which in turn can be seen to prepare the ground and offer practical tools for critically rethinking age(ing). My discussion is based on my main dance practical research method *Solo Partnering*.

---

changing manifestations of our improvised piece *Hoppalappa – Postfolki Tanzi Teateri*. The possibility to make a 'wound' or physical constraint the material or inspirational content for improvising corresponds to Morrish's statement on working with one's own biography.

Dialogue

I suggest that the notion of dialogue is central to improvisatory practice. Landgraf, whose book *Improvisation as Art* engages historically and theoretically with improvisation, defines improvisation as neither a purely individualistic virtuoso practice nor a "celebration of sameness, universality and community" (2011: 12). Instead he proposes that "if we take dialogue and the dynamics of communication, rather then 'community' as a model for improvisational practice, we do not have to think of it in terms of overcoming contradiction and differences, but rather as improvisation exploring the productivity and inventiveness of contentious social processes" (2011: 12). How improvisation practice dialogues inventively and critically with structural and physical constraints is discussed above. I suggest, however, that the dialogues practiced in improvisation in the narrower sense of the word as well take part in preparing the ground for rethinking age(ing).

My practice of *Solo Partnering* serves here as an example for working dialogically. It is a process in which independence and mutual interference, *Eigensinn* (one's own or innate mind, sense and meaning, also indicating obstinacy) and attention for the other, initiating and following meet.[15] As introduced in Chapter I, *Solo Partnering* is a non-hierarchical, self-organised, peer-support practice. During a three-hour long session two partners alternately perform solo improvisation for each other. After verbal exchange about personal interests, needs and possible goals of this day's session and a period of individual or communal warm up, one partner does the first solo, while the other partner is her supportive audience. This is followed by a verbal reflection from the performer, and afterwards, if the performer asks for feedback, from the witness. In the course

---

15 | In this sense I understand this practice to be very close to contact improvisation. However for the sake of clarity and concentration on *Solo Partnering* as my main artistic research practice for this particular inquiry I refrain from deepening the discussion on contact improvisation.

of taking turns performing for one and a half to two hours the solos might deal with tasks, scores or themes; they might build on each other, and might also be influenced by the solos of the partner. In this way, the partners need each other but stay independent in their personal objectives. Both train and reflect upon their individual improvising in relation to their own current artistic goals. They share and sharpen their solo making, and in the dialogic process they allow themselves to be altered by the exchange.

The structure of *Solo Partnering* has space for a substantial amount of difference in objective, in physicality, or in aesthetic preference without weakening the purpose of supporting and stimulating each other. For example, in the course of this research my solo improvising concentrated more and more on age(ing) narratives, yet none of my partners worked with the subject of age(ing). Still, as the following comments reveal, they were able to use *Solo Partnering* as a structure in which they could clarify their own agendas alongside my own.

In order to respect the privacy of my dance partners, the video documentation of *Solo Partnering* contains only examples of my dancing. However, the following statements by some of the partners represent the individuality of their voices and show the diversity of interests and agendas with which the dancers engaged in their own artistic/embodied investigations.[16]

I trained a lot the reflection on "what am I looking at if I see a body in space? What attracts my attention?" [...] Last but not least I used it [one particular session] to help me start to write a text about my work. Carrying the thoughts about that through the whole session I finally talked about it in an improv and did a recording. (Andrea Keiz 2012, personal e-mail)

---

16 | While these quotes show a diversity of agendas and objectives, my practice partners do not represent a wide range of chronological ages. My personal peer group of improvisation practitioners is roughly between 27 and 52 years old.

For me Solo Partnering was a great opportunity to develop and deepen my material for my performance "Übernixung". Even the echo of my material in the other solos and the echo of other material in my improvisations helped me to build connections and to find essences of what I want to say. (Brigitte Kießling 2012, personal e-mail)

The solo-impro practices help me to research in detail some questions about performing, and as well some personal issues about why am I dancing at all! (Mireia Aragones 2012, personal e-mail)

With the proposal to be in a state of awareness, as one would know that they would have to speak of their work immediately after, gave a type of responsibility for the dance. Another positive side to this and what began to weave into the meetings was a type of practice of "discussing" one's practice. So being present and aware whilst dancing/performing and developing a way to speak about one's work. (Shannon Cooney 2012, personal e-mail)

These comments point to how each of these artists has her own individual agenda and process, one that is not compromised by the exchange but rather is sharpened in the dialogue. Keiz's[17] quote shows how *Solo Partnering* can support a clarification process of each partner's current questions, or artistic 'problems'. Kießling[18] makes explicit the individuality and independency of each partner's artistic agenda, whilst also noting mutual inspirations and resonances, which she calls "echoes". What surfaces in Aragones'[19] example is

---

17 | Andrea Keiz is a video artist, improviser and works in the field of video documentation for contemporary dance and live video work in performance. See also: https://vimeo.com/user4886549/videos/all

18 | Brigitte Kießling is an improviser and choreographer and dance teacher. See also: https://brigittekiessling.wordpress.com/

19 | Mireia Aragonès is Alexander Technique teacher, Peak Pilates trainer and dancer. See also: http://mireiaaragones.wix.com/consciousmovement#!about-me/c1me2

that dialogue arises not only between the partners' agendas, or between the singular improvisations that echo each other, but also between the concreteness of what happens in the moment and general questions of artistic motivation and orientation (in her words "why do I dance at all?"). It is up to the partners' interest how much space and explicitness is given to such general questions. The last quote by Cooney[20] communicates how *Solo Partnering* is a space to train a threefold attention:

- Finding and immersing in one's own artistic material of the moment
- Performance awareness, in the sense of studying and developing ways to communicate one's interest and immersion to an audience
- Taking an analytical distance to what was done and seen to be able to verbalise findings and questions

"Discussing" is not meant here as defending or contesting each improvisation but as a reflective tool to search for the next step, to facilitate the next action or idea, to develop action-ability, in other words, agency. Thus, the dialogical principle of *Solo Partnering* offers possibilities for working together with difference and individuality without the necessity for normative homogenisation, which, according to Foster, is still prevalent in many regimes of dance training (Foster 2010).

Reflexivity

Furthermore, I suggest that the quotes above, as well as my solo practice documentation (clip 5-12) demonstrate how these dialogues cultivate reflexivity. I understand the latter as a general mode and disposition to reflect upon one's own doing and thinking and a critical questioning of one's own presumptions, frames of reference, and

---

20 | Shannon Cooney is a dancer, choreographer and teacher in the field of contemporary dance and a craniosacral therapist. See also: http://www.shannoncooney.org/

situatedness (Margarete Sandelowski and Julie Barroso 2002: 216, David Coghlan and Teresa Brannick 2010: 41-43, Gillie Bolton 2010: 13-16).

The improvisation *Walk & Talk* serves as example for the specific reflexive quality that surfaces in *Solo Partnering* (clip 5).[21] Here I first announce the task for my timed six-minute solo as being about warming up my body as well as my concentration "to be able to focus on anything". When the timer marks the end of the solo I reflect with Kießling, my partner in this case, about the significant difference between my presuppositions and my actual doings during this solo. However, reflexivity surfaces not only during the formalised moments of verbal exchange that accompanies each solo, but also during the actual solos. In many of my improvisations during *Solo Partnering* I verbalise my thoughts and experiences during dancing. The following is a transcript of the verbal content of this solo.

It's an observation practice, observing detail. Recognising, recognising – tension – in the neck, tension in the lower back. [...] Recognising, letting be, working with what is there, the body. Enjoying floor instead of showing dance. Trying something without knowing what for. Recognising, letting be. [I gesture towards two pillars in the space] They never go away. I go away, I come back, and I'm 10 seconds older. Working on the position of my pelvis, stretching, not too much, just a little bit, it's a warm up. Not overstretching, just a little bit. Remembering last week Nureyev's diagonal [...]. [Timer beeps to call the end of this improvisation.] Enjoying time

---

21 | To make it easy to navigate the documentation I gave titles to the eight clips I chose from many hours of recorded studio work. I made the titles according to what I consider is the most obvious issue, activity, or feature of each clip. *Walk & Talk* is what I call a 'warm up improvisation', which is the first solo improvisation I perform in front of my witnessing partner in a session. It shows how I give myself a task, then dance, and then reflect together with my partner about the improvisation and the question of warming up.

passing, much more things to do, letting be [end of improvisation]. (Martin 2012, clip 5)

I call this verbalising during dancing reflexive, because it is a complex web of recording observations, assessing associations and possible reactions, and self-instructions. I decide, for example, to not judge ("letting be") my sensations ("tensions in the body") or not to respond to them habitually ("not too much, just a little bit"). The words also recall some key values I appropriated from Morrish's solo practice, which are to "recognise" and to "enjoy" details of my actions and perceptions.[22] This verbalising is aimed at gaining insight into my own improvisational mind as well as sharing my mental process during dancing with my partner in real time.[23] The reiterations in my choice of words also suggest that I am simultaneously activating my compositional awareness and giving the solo a sense of a throughline and form. I suggest that not only this one warm up solo, but all the selected clips exemplify how the strategies of and for this improvisation practice rely on and expand the practitioner's reflexive capacity.

At the end of Chapter II I theorised improvisation as a process oriented practice supporting dancers' agency to probe their individual possibilities in a permanent process of experimentation, exploration and negotiation. I characterised the personhood that emerges in such practice to be unstable, situated, relational, and in process. After having exposed more details of *Solo Partnering* as one specific but not at all uncommon improvisation practice, I propose to add reflexivity to this list of qualities. In other words, it is another implicitly age critical characteristic of improvisation practice to make

---

22 | Since 2003 I have been working periodically with Morrish as coach and mentor for different artistic projects.

23 | A similar emphasis on verbalising experience and thought and can be found in the research practice of de Spain (see for example the article *The Cutting Edge of Awareness* 2003 and the doctoral dissertation *Solo Movement Improvisation* 1997).

space and time for critical self-reflection, contextualising and verbal exchange. Reflexivity can be seen to be one of the basic tools in improvisation to develop an agency of choosing, decision-making, changing, and reacting to change at any point of life. However, I suggest that the reflexivity cultivated in improvisation as well makes such a practice generally less prone to stereotypical categorisations. I expand on this point below.

Practice Tools for Rethinking Age(ing)

The recorded solo improvisations I realised in the dialogical frame of *Solo Partnering* demonstrate that not every aspect of this practice addresses age(ing). The clips show a fuller range of topics and questions being negotiated in solo improvisation. However, they led me to the idea that the reflexivity practiced in improvisation could be base and springboard for rethinking age(ing) beyond stereotypical categorisations. To discuss this idea it is useful to examine *Shift* (clip 12), *Be Obvious* (clip 7), and *What I'm Good In Now* (clip 10) as three more practice examples from *Solo Partnering*. I suggest that each represents a specific reflexive improvisation strategy, which could become a tool for developing a critical stance to age(ing). These are:

- Search for refinement and differentiation in perception and action
- Critique of one's own presumptions and conventions
- Acceptance and activation of one's possibilities here and now

Search for Refinement and Differentiation in Perception and Action

In the clip *Shift* I carry out an improvisation exercise called 'shift', which I learned from Action Theatre performer Sten Rudstrøm.[24] My partner randomly calls 'shift' and I try to react instantly by shift-

---

24 | Sten Rudstrøm performs and teaches in the field of improvisation using voice, movement and language. His work is based in Action Theatre. See also: http://www.stenrudstrom.com/

ing whatever I do at that moment without repeating myself. The exercise reveals that the easiest solution to the task is working with opposition. However, these oppositions quickly lead to a repetitive ping-pong between two stereotypes and the only way out is to break down the perception into more detail. That means it needs the ability to identify the actual complexity inherent in whatever the action to differentiate its components to be able to react in more then just one way. This is all the more difficult when trying to react speedily. With each 'shift' command I try to find new solutions, new interpretations of what a shift can be in relation to my moving body and situation. During a shift exercise I confront my habitual reactions and categories, highlighted by the instantaneousness with which I have to react to the command 'shift'. In other words I push myself, to search for refinement and differentiation in my perceptions and actions. I recognise and try to suspend dualistic stereotypes like shifting between fast and slow, loud and soft, all or nothing. This work, as visible in the video, is not always comfortable and not always successful.[25] However, I suggest it to be an interesting tool for rethinking age(ing) because I train to notice stereotypes and oversimplifications and try to refine and differentiate my perception and action in order to disable them.

Critique of one's own Presumptions and Conventions

Be Obvious is a solo improvisation that took place in the same session as *Walk & Talk,* addressed above. My objective, as in most of the sessions in 2012, is to find my way to enter the subject of age(ing) in my improvising without stopping the particular flow emerging out of each dialogical encounter. In *Be Obvious* I decide to improvise with

---

25 | When I say 'not comfortable or successful' in this context I refer to my subjective experience while improvising but also while watching the video recording of this improvisation. I did not experience a moment of flow (Mihaly Csikszentmihalyi 1990), ease, or a satisfactory feeling of having come to new or surprising solutions for the task, which for me characterise a 'good' improvisation.

the strategies that my solo partner has critically labelled as shallow in her previous improvisation. She feels she has been working with very obvious associations and has followed the first impulse that came to mind and is dissatisfied with this. In reaction to her reflections I decide to work specifically with the obvious and habitual. This challenges not only my partner's intention, but also more generally the intention of many improvisation games, scores and instructions, including the shift exercise in the previous example.[26] By consciously savouring my first and also possibly simplistic and stereotypical impulses I question the conventions that arise from the values of improvisation. In this particular improvisation my decided openness to my first impulse and to the obvious leads me to be less judgemental about repeating themes and images on age(ing) that I have worked with before, such as 'forever young exercises', or 'practicing dying'. Not limiting myself to novelties and a strict notion of inventiveness enables me in this moment to find some kind of flow in letting one association lead into the next, resulting in an improvisation that neither my partner nor I finally experienced to be obvious, shallow, or predictable.[27] My verbal reflection right after, however, reveals the next requirement or convention of improvisation that now I feel to have failed, namely to develop and deepen the ideas that arise instead of jumping from one to the next.

---

26 | As another example Katie Duck's work can be mentioned, known for placing high value on letting the first impulse pass by (personal conversation with the performers Kay Grothusen and Gesine Daniels, former students of Duck). Also Joao Fiadero, with his real time composition system, pays major attention to scrutinize one's decisions before taking action (personal notes during workshop with Fiadero in 2008). For more information on the improvisation-based artists Duck and Fiadero see: http://katieduck.com/; http://www.re-al.org/en/companhia-re-al/

27 | For a theoretical discussion of inventiveness, originality, and innovation in improvisation see Landgraf (2011: 14-41) or Gary Peters (2009: 75-115).

I liked it, I enjoyed it, but I was a little bit, not unhappy, but ... again and again I do these little chunks. So in this nine minutes I make five one and a half minute events, which seems to be what I do easily - to avoid to do something longer. So then again, my critique comes up: *Don't do this little things that you interrupt with speaking, so that you then can start a new little thing.* My working ethos or something is asking to do something that is more sustained and longer, which will make it, in my imagination, more dance – physical – explorative – sensing – than little ideas. [In a joking, authoritarian style:] So I will have to do that in my next improvisation. (Martin 2012, clip 7, min: 11:23)

This clip thus shows how we engage in loops of auto-critique regarding our improvising but also in loops of questioning the values on which we base our judgement, therefore finding forms to critique our own presumptions and conventions. This reflexive tool could as well be used to detect, critique, and playfully rethink my presumptions and conventions regarding age(ing).

Accepting and Activating the Possibilities Here and Now

What I'm Good In Now is an example of the struggle to accept and embrace the claim of working with what is possible here and now.[28] My practice logbook for the session begins with a lament on stress, frustration, arriving late, and time pressure in general. Interestingly, what I then say into my camera and to my witnessing partner, Brenda Waite[29], demonstrates how I re-configure my originally negative state into one that opens up my possibilities and motivation to play with whatever I can come up with here and now. I announce:

---

28 | Working with what is here and now is a basic aspiration in this kind of creative work and basically a variation of the definition of improvisation as extemporaneous composition.

29 | Brenda Waite is an improviser, live-art performer, and clown. See also: http://brendawaite.blogspot.de/

Just right now I thought: I have a list here with lots of things I never could do. I have another big list with lots of things I cannot do anymore. And then there is a small list with things I still can do. No - let's say it differently. There's a list of things I never could do, there's a list of things I cannot do anymore right now, and there's a list of things I'm fantastically good in. So let's do the things I'm fantastically good in and forget about the other lists. (Martin 2012, clip 10)

In this short moment of improvised speech I am pushing myself to mentally and emotionally re-open, affirming possibilities, agency and general appreciation of my abilities. I decide to focus on what is available here and now, without knowing yet what that is and what I will do in this particular improvisation. Important here is that I catch myself in projecting my acute frustrations and arduousness onto my life-story, limiting my future according to the normative age script of diminishing capabilities and the long list of things I can no longer do versus the short list of things I still can do. In reaction I spontaneously reword my self-description in exactly the way proposed in Gullette's concept of age autobiography (discussed in Chapter II). In retrospect I still do not know if I am more led by my improviser's knowledge that such negative imagery is unhelpful, or by my growing age critical awareness, which tells me to interrupt the impulse of judging and narrating my life as one of incessant loss and decay. What can be stated is that these two levels of awareness overlap in this moment and offer me a way out of frustration and into a productive practice session. Or, to paraphrase the quote of Morrish earlier, I realise that what I can do is actually what is relevant to me as an improviser. Therefore reflexively accepting and activating the possibilities here and now presents itself in this particular improvisation clearly as a practice tool for rethinking age(ing).

Thus, considering all three examples I suggest that improvisation practice can offer tools that support our noticing of stereotypes and oversimplifications as well as strategies for deconstructing or disabling them. The practice encourages dancers to suspend binary conceptions of self and others, and to be open and able to disrupt their own norms and habits. These reflexive strategies are not only valuable for developing a satisfying improvisation practice. They further offer an actual and practical toolbox that can help to put the age critical objectives analysed in Chapter II into practice, namely:

- To subvert stereotypical representations of age(ing)
- To suspend dichotomist conceptions of age(ing)
- And to disrupt ageist cultural norms

In other words, to actually rethink age(ing) it is useful to hone one's reflexive and deconstructive capacities and tools and improvisation is a practice that does this. However, dancers who practice such forms of experimental auto-critique and norm-critique are not automatically aware and critical of the ageist cultural norms that surround them. Neither is it a given that improvising dancers are always ready to face and question their own ageist norms, or the ageism they might foster against themselves. Given that age(ing) does not pose such a big problem in improvisation as in more formalised dance forms, it might be possible that age(ing) is hardly thought about and therefore also not subject to critical reflection. Nevertheless, as I have shown, the reflexive strategies and tools of improvisation can strengthen an age critical consciousness and an age critical dance practice. Indeed, in my emergent research process that is what happened. I kept scrutinising age(ing) in and through my reflexive practice of *Solo Partnering* to finally select and rework some of my critical improvisations on age(ing) into the *Fountain* pieces. By doing that I activated the implicit age critique and reflexivity I identify in improvisation practice and applied it as a tool to further what I call my explicitly age critical performance practice, which is addressed in the following chapter.

SUMMARY

The preceding chapter discusses a range of implicitly age critical practice features of improvisation that are informative for rethinking age(ing) in dance. It demonstrates how improvisation focuses on open-ended explorative and reflexive processes and thereby offers alternative ways of attending to and doing age(ing) beyond the static dichotomies of youth and age. The chapter first attends to what I call the building of microstructures for sustained artistic practice. Improvisers' engagement in building alternative and peer-supportive microstructures at the margin of a competitive and youth oriented professional field enables them to skirt the structural constraints shaping dance and to sustain their artistic practice past early midlife. The second section analyses how it is integral to improvisational practices to also develop ways of dealing with shifting physical constraints. Neither the body nor the arts practice is understood and expected to be static. Dealing with change and searching for creative ways of working with and through constraint as well includes the consequences of functional age(ing). Consequently, I suggest the engagement in sustainable microstructures as well as the negotiation of shifting physical constraints to be both implicitly age critical as they refute the naturalised progress-peak-decline narrative and the supposed youthful nature of dance discussed in the previous chapter. The final section of this chapter argues that improvisation is a dialogical practice. A close reading of *Solo Partnering* further suggests that what is developed in the dialogues of improvisation is a high degree of reflexivity and thus a dancer's capacity to critically examine her artistic making and the conventions and presumptions on which she bases her practice. Improvisation as a practice to hone ones reflexive and deconstructive capacities can thus be seen to offer some basic but important tools for an age critical dance practice. Where I find age(ing) to be addressed more explicitly than in the working structures, strategies, and inquiries of improvisation practice is in moments of theatrical performance. It is consequently the age critical potential of performance making that I turn to in the following chapter.

IV. Performing Age(ing)

Introduction

This fourth and last chapter focuses on the possibility of dance to contribute to a critical age(ing) discourse through purposefully and explicitly addressing age(ing) in performance. It argues that critical representations, images and narratives of age(ing), developed for the stage and shared with audiences, are crucial for rethinking age(ing) in and through dance. For if the publicly staged performance works continue to reiterate stereotypical narratives of age(ing), then implicitly critical practices and the individually sustainable working structures, such as those developed by improvisation practitioners discussed in Chapter III, only have a limited ability to inspire changes in our understanding of age(ing). Or, as Butler states: "The formulation of the body as a mode of dramatizing or enacting possibilities offers a way to understand how a cultural convention is embodied and enacted" (1988: 525). I suggest that it is not by chance that Butler uses the vocabulary of theatre. Artistic performances have the unique potential to make explicit how cultural conventions are embodied and enacted and, in turn, how to play with the scope of possibility and variation therein.

Accordingly, this chapter first highlights the alternative and imaginative dramatisations or enactments of age(ing) in the work of selected dance artists. I draw on data that is either statements of artists, who position their own performance works in relation to discourses of age(ing), or theatrical performances that address age(ing). I also draw on two *artistic responses to age(ing)* (clip 20, 21), which I consider to be one-to-one artistic performances carried out specifically for this research. The second section discusses my own attempts towards age critical performance making, called *Performing Age(ing)*, with specific reference to *The Fountain of Youth* and *The Fountain of Age* as the two main stage works developed within the framework of this research.

Thus my debate on age(ing) in this chapter moves away from the content of Chapter III and its discussion of the age critique implicit in the processes and practices of improvisation. Rather, it focuses on performance strategies and explicitly age critical positions articulated in and for the moment of performance no matter the role or degree of improvisation in each particular work staged. Also in regard to my own performances it is not my intention to elaborate on the making process and the steps between the process of *Solo Partnering* and the finished 'products' of the *Fountain* pieces. Such extended discussion on artistic making processes, though interesting, would move me away from my interest in the actual age narratives and images realised on stage. However, some evidence of the making process of the *Fountain* pieces is available through the video documentation (clip 13-14).

NEGOTIATING AGE(ING) IN CURRENT PERFORMANCE MAKING

Current performance works that focus principally on debates on age(ing) can be roughly divided into two groups: pieces choreographed for a special cast of older performers, and pieces in which performers/choreographers produce works that address age(ing) by using their own bodies.[1] Noteworthy examples that fall into the first category include the following works: *Kontakthof mit Damen und Herren ab 65* (Kontakthof with Ladies and Gentlemen over 65) by Pina Bausch (2000), which reconstructs the piece *Kontakthof* origi-

---

1 | With 'current performance works' I refer to works made and performed between 2000 and 2015.

nally made for and with Bausch's company in 1978 for a cast of older people who previously have not been involved in theatre dance.[2] Further, *Gardenia* by Alain Platel and Frank van Laecke (2010) is about the last performance of a travesty cabaret. The majority of the cast is 55+ and many of the performers are actual travesty performers. In *Alte Liebe* (*Old Love*) by Britta Pudelko (2010) four former ballerinas reevaluate their past and present relationship to dance, juxtaposed by a *Jungmännerchor* (young men's choir), a movement chorus of twelve young men. *Come Back* by Doris Uhlig (2013) stages, similar to *Alte Liebe*, former ballet dancers, who approach questions of agency, body, society and personal narrative. There is also *The Elders Project* by Jonathan Burrows and Matteo Fargion (2014). This production invites to the stage a cast of older dancers with different stylistic backgrounds and explores how to represent them as individuals with particular body, and dance-histories.[3]

Such works are relevant within the context of this research primarily because they use older bodies as their inspiration and as material for choreography. However, although they give visibility to older dancers and partly offer non-normative representations of age, such productions nevertheless also risk reiterating the limited agency of age(ing) performers critiqued in the Introduction. Whilst such pieces acknowledge the various contributions of the dancers to these works, they tend to follow the traditional choreographer-performer divide, which in varying degrees can place the dancers in a disadvan-

---

2 | In 2008 Kontakthof has been as well reconstructed with teenagers over 14. Both productions gave raise to interesting documentary films by Lilo Mangelsdorff (2002) and Anne Linsel and Rainer Hoffmann (2009).

3 | Confirming the growing attention for questions of age(ing) and for older dancers, discussed in Chapter II, *The Elders Project* was commissioned by the new London dance event, the *Elixir Festival* at Sadler's Wells, London, a "four day festival, celebrating lifelong creativity and the contribution of older artists, including performances, workshops and a full day conference" (festival blog). For more information on the *Elixir Festival* and *The Elders Project* see: http://rescen.net/blog_elix/?page_id=57

taged position. The cases mentioned were one-off productions, implying that the performers were cast according to the needs of this specific project without offering a continuing work environment for these dancers. This is not to suggest that the mentioned choreographers are unaware of the problems that ageing dancers face; on the contrary, these works offer one possible way to reflect upon the issues of ageing and dancing on stage. Another interesting initiative is *Dance On*, a new repertory company for dancers above 40 that started their work in 2015. Similar to the concept of Nederlands Dans Theater III the mission of this company with six dancers is "to show how dance as an art form benefits from experienced dancers" (Dance On website). Time will tell if this ensemble can establish itself beyond the initial project phase of two years.

However, the focus of my research is on the second category of performance making, namely on those artists who reflect age(ing), and who allow their audiences to reflect age(ing) by staging their own bodies in negotiation with age(ing) and an ageist culture. These artists continue to attend to their age(ing) bodies as a base and medium for their creativity (as discussed in Chapter III). In turn, they sustain a stage presence throughout many years and many different pieces. This offers the audience the possibility to follow an articulation of dance that necessarily changes over time and in parallel with the changes in the artists' body. Even more importantly, the artists discussed in the following also use their embodied art to create explicitly critical representations of age(ing).

Performance makers who explicitly and critically address their own age(ing) realities and fantasies on stage and use their own bodies as performance material include: Marc Tompkins in the solo *Song and Dance* (2003); Thomas Langkau and Yoshiko Waki in their duet *Schwund (Atrophy)* from 2004, taken up again in 2011 under the title *Forever Young*; Yvonne Rainer in *Trio A: Geriatric With Talking* from 2010; Wendy Houstoun in her solo performances *50 Acts* (2011) and *Pact with Pointlessness* (2014); Liz Aggiss in *The English Channel* (2014a); and Morrish in several untitled solo improvisations and in his improvisation for the performance series *Unter Uns – Das*

Generationenprojekt (2012) (*Between Us – The Generation Project*) by Silke Z.[4] I include furthermore the two *artistic responses to age(ing)* by Crisp (2012) and Morrish (2014a) performed specifically for this research project. The discussion that follows is based on the work of these artists and their public statements and elaborates three key approaches to explicit age critique in performance. These are:

- Resisting the youthfulness of dance
- Reconciling with age(ing) and death
- Colliding with age norms

Resisting the Youthfulness of Dance

For older dancers, continuing to perform into midlife is still not a matter of course, and, whilst not a main focus of this book, this is especially true for women. For even if a dancer maintains a physiologically 'dance-able' body, or what age studies and gerontology would call biologically or functionally young, she still has to negotiate what Woodward (2006: 183) calls cultural age (see Chapter II). One such negotiation strategy is that of explicitly enunciating and resisting a (dance) cultural youth orientation. Houstoun, for example, writes about herself in the following way: "Her performance style still retains a hallmark of honesty, humour and vulnerability and she continues to perform her own work while negotiating the complexities of ageing in a youth focused discipline" (2013: unpaginated).[5] I suggest that the stated qualities 'honesty, humour and vulnerability' cannot be read independently from the second half of this statement, that is, the part that addresses age(ing). These terms also

---

4 | There are many more artists that cannot be addressed in this research, like, for example, Halprin, mentioned already in Chapter II. Age related works by her include *Still Dance with Anna Halprin* in collaboration with Eeo Stubblefield (1997 – 2000) and *Intensive Care* (2000).

5 | For more information about the work of Houstoun see: http://www.wendyhoustoun.net/

signify actual artistic, aesthetic, personal strategies that react to the dominant cultural devaluation of age(ing) (female) dancers. Honesty and exposing vulnerability in terms of one's own age(ing) body can be seen as resisting normative expectations. Woodward argues, for example, that "the normative youth-old age system and sex-gender system" makes demands on women to "invest themselves in passing for younger, concealing their bodies in a masquerade of youth" (2006: 167).[6] The honesty of not trying to pass as younger, therefore, goes hand in hand with an increased vulnerability of being rejected as a dancer and as a woman. At the same time, however, this strategy widens our cultural images and imaginations of age(ing) and older dancers and is therefore what I call explicitly age critical.

Not trying to pass for younger, exposing vulnerability and showing humour by disclosing possible contradictions and ambiguities of age(ing), as well as unconventional age images and "the willingness to look a fool now and then" (Houstoun 2013: unpaginated), characterise Houstoun's age critical performance strategies and aesthetics. Moreover, her works embody Woodward's argument against the cooled down and withdrawn attitude that is connected with old age wisdom, expressing at times what can be called an angry energy. Dance critic Judith Mackrell, for example, describes Houstoun in her solo *50 Acts* to "rant against the tyranny of Botox and beige", to test "the powers of language to dissipate the nonsense of a culture obsessed with youth" and the show to cover "a gamut of reasons why a woman over 50 might be angry" (2012: unpaginated). However, Mackrell stresses as well that the performed anger is embedded in the clownish and surreal aesthetic of the piece.

Aggiss, as another example, defines her work in her artistic portfolio as: "attend[ing] to the transgressive, subversive, expressive, aging and fleshy body that exceeds expectations of what 'this' particular dancing body should be doing and where she should be doing it,

---

6 | Woodward's analysis echoes Sontag's concept of the double standard of ageing as discussed in Chapter II, but also the seminal article on the performance of femininity by Joan Riviere: *Womenliness as Masquerade* (1929).

whilst developing live routes that push boundaries of presentation within conventional dance practice" (Aggiss 2014b: unpaginated).[7] Aggiss describes her body/a body through a series of attributes. Applying an age theoretical perspective, I would paraphrase her by stating: it is the not-so-young fleshiness of the body that collides with the expectations and boundaries not only of conventional dance practice, but also of our wider culture. Thus Aggiss' explicitly age critical performance strategy is to blatantly and humorously present precisely this collision of her actual body with the stereotypes circulating and encouraged in the dance world. Or, as critic Lara Burns would have it: "Aggiss' *The English Channel* is a celebration of defiance, of not sitting down quietly, of asserting an identity that refuses to be categorised" (2014: unpaginated).

Rainer, in contrast, creates critical friction, not by relating to any mainstream images of female dancing bodies, but by reevaluating her own ideals of avant-garde dance from the 1960s in relation to her current body. In 2010, she created a new version of her 1966 signature solo piece *Trio A*, retitling it *Trio A: Geriatric With Talking*. In her article "The Aching Body in Dance" (2014), she reflects on this piece and her recent choreographic work since returning to dance in 2000.[8] In this instance she most certainly employs the qualities of honesty, humour and vulnerability that Houstoun speaks of. Discussing her work *Trio A: Geriatric with Talking*, Rainer says:

> I would like you to think of this version of *Trio A* not as evidence of deterioration and decline, but as a new form of avant-garde dance. The aging body is a thing unto itself and need not be judged as inadequate or inferior if it can no longer jump through hoops. In fact, the evolution of the aging body

---

7 | For more information on the work of Aggiss see: http://www.lizaggiss.com
8 | Rainer left the dance world around 1974 to focus on experimental narrative filmmaking. She picked up choreographing again via a commission from the White Oak Dance Project in 2000. See also her autobiography *Feelings are Facts* (2006). Under the same title a documentary film by Jack Walsh premiered at the Berlin film festival in 2015.

in dance fulfils the earliest aspirations of my 1960s peers and colleagues who tore down the palace gates of high culture to admit a rabble of alternative visions and options. Silence, noise, walking, running, detritus – all undermined prevailing standards of monumentality, beauty, grace, professionalism, and the heroic. It is high time to admit the aging body of the dancer into this by now fully recognized and respected universe. Aging is the ultimate goal and hurdle, one that I myself must confront. So I tell myself, Yvonne, keep on reading your texts, but continue to dance, aches and all. Farewell to mewling "I no longer dance." Dance, girl, dance, and to all who observe me, I challenge you, "Pity me not." Granted, I shall need a little empathy from my friends. (Rainer 2014: 6)

What Rainer manages to articulate that I would call explicitly age critical are the multiple aspects of age(ing) that, together, manifest as a hurdle, even though mainstream (dance) culture is not her point of reference. The complex mix that Rainer negotiates is the memory of her own past self, her past physical capabilities, her current pains, aches and limitations, and how to redefine her present-day aesthetic standards.

For Aggiss, Houstoun, and Rainer their emancipatory attempts to resist the cultural devaluation of age(ing) in dance comprise of insisting on not passing but instead on challenging the narrow conventions of dance (Aggiss), focussing on vulnerability and honesty as virtue rather then weakness (Houstoun), and exploring the possibility of stiff and arduous movements of an aged body as an interesting and valuable quality in dance (Rainer).

Reconciling with Age(ing) and Death

The next section deals with artists who place their sensual experiencing of a time bound bodily existence at the forefront. I read this as a reconciliatory attitude towards age(ing) and death. For example, Crisp offers what I see as a poetic way of performing a positive take on age(ing). Normally her public performances do not address the subject of age(ing), but she responds to the issue after being invited to create an artistic response to a range of age(ing) related keywords I had prepared for her in January 2012 (clip 20).[9] In response to *Beautifully Old – Beautifully Young* she choses to dance and speak at once in a probing and reflective manner, as if testing her own body and her current sensations in response to the words given to her. She states:

Old is beautiful because you are full of. You have more sensations. More permissions and more bits in your body. That's the thing that happened to me. That's what is more beautiful about the older body, the older bodies I see. They have got more bits. [Martin: What's bits? Pieces?] Bits. You've been in parts of the body, you've been in them, because they have been touched or hit or sat on, or knocked or kissed. Yeah, as I said, you got more bits. I think that's beautiful about being old. (Crisp 2012, clip 20, min 5:00)

What is interesting here is that Crisp deliberately maintains a certain openness and vagueness to what she means by 'bits' and to whose 'bits' she is referring. In doing so she avoids fixing any exact location or value to them. She remains playful and explorative with regards to her movements, her imagination and the subject matter of age(ing), allowing for a flexible interpretation of the 'bits'. This short improvisation on *Beautifully Old – Beautifully Young* specifically illustrates Crisp's understanding of dance as well as age(ing), and the life course more generally as a practice or an ongoing creative process. Indeed, for Crisp the age(ing) body is something to be moving in/with/from with active interest. Exploring the detail in the awareness

---

9 | As already mentioned in Chapter I, the keywords I decided for her are: Living and Dead Bones; Beautifully Old – Beautifully Young; Morbid Wisdom; Experience that leads to … …; Weakness, Stiffness, Tiredness; Post Menopause – The Witch; Career – Visibility – Recognition. Chapter I explains as well the broader function and intention of *artistic responses to age(ing)*.

and usage of one's 'bits', one's sensations is for her the task as well as the gain of age(ing).

Morrish's work exemplifies yet another way of evoking non-stereotypical representations of age(ing). In his untitled solo performed on 1 August 2013 during the festival Improvisation Xchange Berlin,[10] he improvised a piece during which he rehearses his own death by performing horizontality, stillness, letting go, and nothingness. In not affirming verticality or movement, his imagery diverges from the traditional notion of dance as an art form, representing liveliness through sparky, animated activity. His imagery is also diametrically opposed to the uplifting or energising idea of the health benefits of dance, which is dominant in the age(ing) discourses of medical research, community dance, movement and dance therapy. While I am not arguing against dance's proven positive effects on health and wellbeing[11] I see Morrish's approach to hint at an additional potential of dance, namely to improve our imagination of or preparedness for dying. Morrish's attempt to 'practice' dying furthermore resonates with Deborah Hay's concept of "the whole body of a dancer exploring dying" (Hay 1994: xi).[12] As Hay explains:

---

10 | For more information on this improvisation festival see: http://www.berlinartsunited.com/

11 | Neuroscience in particular run studies on the health effects of dancing. See for example the work of the *Neural Plasticity Lab* at Ruhr-University Bochum, Germany http://www.neuralplasticitylab.de/index.aspx?culture=EN and in particular the work of Kattenstroth et al. (2013, 2011).

12 | Morrish's and Hay's relating to death resonates as well with Foucault's thinking about death. Discussing the practices and exercises described by ancient Greek philosopher Seneca he writes: "At the pinnacle of all these exercises there is the famous *melete thanatou* - meditation on, or rather, training for death. In fact it does not consist in a simple, albeit insistent, reminder that one will die. It is a way of making death actual in life. [...] It aims to ensure that one lives each day as if it were the last. [...] What gives the meditation on death its particular value is not just that it anticipates what opinion generally represents as the greatest misfortune; it is not just

"I am making an effort to come to terms with dying as an experiential process of which I possess negotiable comprehension. I want to include the perception of dying in my performance practice because it invigorates my living each moment" (Hay 1994: xi).[13]

Apart from this correspondence, Morrish's performance style is indeed different from Hay's work. While Hay develops long and detailed scores for her dances she calls 'movement librettos' (1994: xii) Morrish does not approach a predecided theme, or subject matter, nor does he create scores for his solo works. Instead, he performs with a high degree of openness and interest in the instantaneous discovery of congruities in an improvisation. Or, using the language of improviser Nancy Stark Smith, his interest lies in the discovery of confluences, divergencies and coincidences. Yet, both artists use the consciousness of their own mortality as inspiration and a valuable source for shaping a performance. They articulate positions towards age(ing) and mortality that counter the celebration of youthfulness conventionally expected of dance. This can also be seen in Morrish's *artistic response to age(ing),* performed for this research (clip 21). In this performance, he speaks about death and grace. He uses the example of a terminally ill woman, someone who participated in and danced with him in a dance therapy group.

She always knew exactly how long the dance was, whereas before she never knew when to finish. She always knew exactly the right energy to have, the energy she had, whereas before she was always pushing, like a physical education teacher. Suddenly she says: This is it, this is my dance.

---

that it enables one to convince oneself that death is not an evil; rather, it offer possibilities of looking back, in advance so to speak, on one´s life. By considering oneself as at the point of death, one can judge the proper value of every action one is performing" (Foucault 2005: 504-505).

13 | For more information on Hay's work see for example: http://www.deborahhay.com For more information on her thinking on death see also *Autobiography in the Present Tense: Deborah Hay, Living and Dying At Once* by Leslie Satin (1999).

This is it. And then it would be finished. I stopped breathing many times watching her dance because of the grace. No effort, no push, just a single, simple statement: This is it. This is all I have to say. I'm not frustrated, I'm not bored, I'm not proud, I'm not apologising. This is all I have to say. I'm not ashamed. This is all I have to say. [...] It was so fucking beautiful that she knew that's all there was. (Morrish 2014a, clip 21, min 9:46)

Morrish performs his response to age(ing) in this solo with both lightness and urgency. Clearly, it is important for him that the audience recognises that age(ing) brings us closer to death, and that we all, individually, have to come to terms with this. He also emphasises the experience of beauty and grace in connection with death and, in doing so, makes a point of detaching both these terms from representations of youthful athletic bodies, balletic elegance, or the promise of a future.

Together Crisp, Hay, and Morrish all point to the relevance of a corporeal self no longer young and recognising its mortality. Crisp addresses age(ing) in relation to gaining experience and awareness of discernible sensations; Hay acknowledges death as invigorating; and finally Morrish proposes the process of practicing a graceful death both on and off stage. In the context of this research I name this stance a reconciliatory one. Each of these artists has a very unique way of discovering something meaningful in the process of age(ing) or dying. By radically valuing the old body, mortality, and/or death in performance, these artists open up the possibility to reconcile themselves and their audience with the challenges of age(ing). I suggest that to be another way of staging a more explicit critique of a culture that, in its orientation towards youth and a meritocratic ideology, gets more and more estranged from the end of life, which is death.

While all three artists share a positive notion of age, it can be argued that they do so without following a simple age as progress or age as wisdom ideology, which I critiqued in Chapter II. A progress or seniority narrative (Gullette 2004: 14-20) as well as the emotional detachment and superiority of wisdom (Woodward 2002: 206), while possibly conveying more positive connotations than decline, nevertheless perpetuates a binary and fixed understanding of one's life course. It also implies the idea of gaining or possibly missing to gain a specific identity of being senior or being wise. I understand reconciliation, in contrast, not as an age identity but as a relationship to age(ing). Such an active relationship can also be dynamic and inconsistent. It allows the artists to develop possibly ambiguous, complex and idiosyncratic readings and representations of age(ing) and death beyond a static idea of what a good or meaningful age(ing) process should contain.

Colliding with Age Norms

Two specific performances, one of Tompkins and one of Langkau and Waki illustrate another critical representation of age(ing). These artists work with self-parody and evoke the ridiculous and absurd by letting their bodies collide with normative values and imagery in dance (Langkau and Waki) or pop culture (Tompkins). They play with their past, future and fictitious selves when performing ridiculous dreams or embarrassing memories. Through such humorous self-exposure they explicitly stress the impossibility of resolving the collision between individual experience and surrounding normative expectations, or incorporated values and desires.

Tompkins' solo *Song and Dance* (2003) is a dream-like piece about the artifice of the stage, depicting the aftermath of a (fictitious) show.[14] While the technicians are dismantling the set, the performer surrenders to fantasies and memories, invents fictitious divas, embraces a skeleton for a dance of death, performs the morbid, nostalgic, ridiculous, romantic, and absurd selves that could neither be given space in the 'real' performance, nor in everyday life. His piece is further structured through a chain of iconic and nostalgic songs such as *Stairway to Heaven* (Led Zeppelin) or *My Way* (originally

---

14 | For more information on *Song and Dance* and the work of Tompkins see: http://www.idamarktompkins.com/?q=en/songanddance_english

by Anka/Francois/Revaux, but popularised by Frank Sinatra) and plays with the ghosts and shadows of finality, dying, and vulnerability. Tompkins employs a mix of intimate self-exposure and irony and stresses the performativity of age(ing) and gender by playfully exaggerating the means of theatre. Early on in the performance he removes for instance his eighteenth-century costume tights to reveal an upholstered jockstrap and fake leg muscles incorporated into the tights. Yet, despite his witty and ironic exposure of theatricality and illusions on and off stage, Tompkins refrains from positioning himself as someone age(ing) into wisdom and self-sufficient detachment or into reconciliation, but instead remains the whimsical clown who always wanted to be a rock star.

Similarly, *Forever Young* (2004/2011) by Langkau and Waki offers a biographical, self-mocking, ironic age narrative.[15] The performers mercilessly use their personal histories as dancers as well as their physical injuries and constraints to address a dearth of prospects for age(ing) dancers. Exposing their intimate attempts and failures to reconcile with a corporeal self, one that is no longer young, they perform the tale of their lives/careers as having missed the moment to gracefully choreograph their own stage death. As a result, they reiterate aesthetics from the past and emulate movements their bodies execute only with resistance. It is as if they are stuck in a loop, appearing again and again like 'the undead', making yet another 'last' piece, and a 'last' performance.

I call both pieces explicitly age critical not only because they articulate the collision with normative expectations but also for their articulation of the impossibility of resolution with regards to defining the self, the limits of dance, or death. Akin to my own performance practice, they do this by working with parody, which is defined, according to literary theorist Linda Hutcheon, as "repetition, but repetition that includes difference (Deleuze 1968); it is imitation with critical ironic distance" (1985: 37). These artists approach

---

15 | For more information on *Forever Young* and the work of Langkau and Waki see: http://www.bodytalkonline.de/

age(ing) by imitating their own ideal or former selves, while at the same time emphasising the gap between their imaginations and their actual bodies. They perform a failing to reconcile with age(ing) by exposing experiences of loss, disappointment, and nostalgia. However, the well functioning dramaturgy of seriousness and absurdity, of humour that arouses empathy, of virtuosic quoting, knowingly appropriating and imperfectly reiterating dominant images from Western dance and performance culture, positions them as effective and convincing performers whose artistic tools actually do not rely on brilliant dance moves. Similar to the discussion in the previous chapter on Eriksson's use of her 'wounds' and Morrish's use of his biography as material to improvise from and with, these artist's losses are their content material to work with, and thereby not (anymore) impediments.

In short, no matter if openly resisting ageism in dance, performing reconciliatory approaches to individual age(ing) process, or staging an absurd, clownish age(ing) self in collision with an ageist (dance) culture, all performers mentioned in this section insist on continuing to perform beyond their thirties and forties. Moreover, they also dare to stage age(ing) as a subject matter, based on and inspired by their own rich histories and experiences as dancers, bodies, and people; revealing subjectivities on stage that are vulnerable, changing and mortal. Such performances accomplish what age theorists Gullette (2004: 159-178) and Woodward (2006) acknowledge to be the special potential of performing arts; namely to imagine and stage alternative and irritating representations of age(ing), through which the meanings of age and gender can be retold, subverted, and performed differently.[16] In other words, they all engage with explicitly age critical performance making.

---

16 | This idea is as well discussed in more recent publications like for example in Lipscomb and Marshall's *Staging Age (2010)*, Michael Mangan's *Staging Ageing* (2013), and Swinnen and John A. Stotesbury's *Aging, Performance and Stardom* (2012).

The next section considers my own approach to explicitly age critical performance. My artistic engagement with age(ing) shows yet a different route from those discussed above, as my work tries to preclude any definite stance in relation to age(ing) and instead promotes strategically ambiguous age narratives in performance.

PERFORMING AGE(ING) – A PERFORMANCE PRACTICE

This section addresses my performance practice *Performing Age(ing)*, which is comprised of a series of performance works I have authored since 2003. All of these pieces centrally question age(ing). The name itself, however, was formed in relationship to the process of writing this book and more specifically through discussing *The Fountain of Youth* (2013) and *The Fountain of Age* (2015) as the latest works of this series. I first introduce *Performing Age(ing)* in more general terms and then move to a discussion of some of its artistic strategies in more detail, that is, by discussing specific aspects of *The Fountain of Youth* and *The Fountain of Age*.

Performing Age(ing) distinguishes itself from the dance works discussed thus far in part because of its long-term focus on the theme of age(ing). It is a continuing artistic engagement and a deconstructive practice that, as a whole, emphasises contradictory and continuously changing perspectives, experiences, narratives, and meanings of age(ing). Furthermore, in *Performing Age(ing)* the dancer and audience's reflections on age(ing) is not instigated by or constructed around an already chronologically and functionally old body, as is the case in the late work of Rainer (born 1934), Halprin (born 1920) or Kazuo Ohno (born 1906). Instead, I have been continuously developing *Performing Age(ing)* since 2003 (when I was thirty-five years old) from the perspective of a midlife dancer. *Performing Age(ing)* proposes that age(ing) is a subject that can be reflected upon and addressed artistically by artists and audiences of any chronological age. It shows that this discourse is neither bound to a senior audience nor to exceptionally old dancers on stage. Instead the different works comprising *Performing Age(ing)* suggest that we all, and at any time, are confronted with cultural expectations, imaginations and narratives of age(ing), that we all, and at any chronological age, react to and relate to our age(ing) culture. *Performing Age(ing)* examines how to fulfil the expectations, reiterate the narratives, and how to deconstruct them. This is meaningful since even researchers who discuss the arts and theatre's potential to offer a critique or alternative against ageist stereotypes tend to focus their interest on art works that feature people of over sixty years of age (for example Woodward 2006, Swinnen 2012, or Kaplan 2010).

The Performance Works of Performing Age(ing)

Since starting *Performing Age(ing)* I had explored the subject of age(ing) from a multitude of perspectives and through a range of performance works, such as *Herr K. Müh* (2003), *Claudia* (2004), *JULIO* (2006), and *Rosi tanzt Rosi* (2007-2009). These works both precede and inform my current Practice as Research inquiry and its performance articulations *The Fountain of Youth* and *The Fountain of Age*, which I now summarise in more detail.

The 45-minute solo *The Fountain of Youth* that premiered in Gothenburg, Sweden, plays with the notion of eternal youth and presents a collection of related findings, revelations, and practices on the concept. It brings together a selection of ideas developed in and through *Solo Partnering*, my main improvisation and research practice in relationship to this research.[17] Structurally, *The Fountain of Youth* is divided into seven scenes, each offering a different way to address age(ing). Each scene is visually and verbally titled. The titles are:

- Forever Young Exercises
- Improvisation and Dementia

---

17 | First drafts of some scenes have also appeared in informal research showings and in the frame of the performance series *Susi & Gabi's Salon*.

- Looking Back – Looking Forward
- Still Dancing
- Nostalgia
- Balls & Energy
- The Doc Martin Forever Young Meta Method

The Fountain of Youth, Gothenburg (2013)

IV. Performing Age(ing)   141

Photos: Lars Åsling

In terms of movement and stage presence, I present myself as a professional performer and researcher on age(ing), neither young nor old, with movement qualities and choreographic strategies informed by improvisation. I play with ambiguity by layering and juxtaposing movement, text, music and costuming in ways that blur the lines between truth and lie, artifice and informality, parody and empathy, dancing and lecturing. In doing so, my aim is to unsettle the audience in any preconceived notions of how best to understand and deal with the question of age(ing).

Similarly, the 35-minute solo *The Fountain of Age* is a collage of scenes in which dance, text, costume, mask work, and music interrelate. This piece once more references the image of the fountain, here indicating that the subject of age(ing) has been and continues to be a delightful source of inspiration for my dance making.[18]

---

18 | *The Fountain of Age* is the title of a book by Betty Friedan. Her book is an example of a feminist culture-critical publication on age(ing) that received wider public attention in the US and in Europe. In the preface she explains the title as such: "I came to realize that the fountain of age didn't

The Fountain of Age reviews the extended series of works that have emerged throughout *Performing Age(ing)* and that I have outlined earlier. It is thus a performance that summarises and reflects upon my own past and future performances on age. In quick succession, the piece presents an opera style stage death, and revives the aged male social dancer *K. Müh*, the female chair dancer *Claudia*, and the cross-generational dance diva *Rosi*. Much like *The Fountain of Youth*, each scene, as well as the piece as a whole, tells an ambiguous tale of age(ing) to counteract any simple ascertainment of age(ing). Through quickly changing masks, costumes, time references, and enacted roles, this solo plays with the multiplicity of my personal age selves as well as a sense of taking a journey through time.

The Fountain of Age, London (2015)

---

mean, can't mean, the absence of physiological, emotional, or situational change. But it takes so much effort to hold on to the illusion of youth, to keep the fear of age at bay, that in doing so we could fail to recognize the new qualities and strengths that might emerge" (1994: 28).

IV. Performing Age(ing) 143

Photos: William Gillingham-Sutton

Obviously, ambiguity, when understood as a playful, reflexive attitude towards genre conventions and audience expectations, is not unique to the *Fountain* pieces or to *Performing Age(ing)*. It is a feature of much contemporary performance and has been discussed, for example, by theatre scholar Lehmann. He argues ambiguity is "the unsettling that occurs through the *indecidability* whether one is dealing with reality or fiction" (2006: 101). Lehmann discusses this kind of ambiguity to be one of the defining features of what he calls postdramatic theatre. In a related fashion, but with a more specific emphasis on the embodied experiences of dancing and watching dance, Claid makes ambiguity the leitmotiv for her analysis of performer-spectator relations, and discusses ambiguity as the multiplicity of meaning that a dancing body can evoke for the spectator. Both researchers' discussions resonate strongly with the issues foregrounded in the Fountain pieces, because they articulate the specific reflexivity that can be mobilised in and through performances. Claid, for example, helpfully highlights the activity of the audience when engaging in what I would call 'reflexive spectating'. "Our work as spectators is to remember the conventions and codes but not to be fixed by them. We know we can engage in a play of not knowing but desiring to know. We let go of the desire for fixed meanings but search for meanings all the same" (Claid 2006: 206).

In line with Claid and Lehmann I understand such reflexive spectating to evolve alongside similarly reflexive, deconstructive ways of performances making and performers who create "undecidability" (Lehmann 2006: 101) and engage in becoming "the surface for ambiguity to play" (Claid 2006: 204). I can easily identify my performance practice as part of a lineage of works these writers discuss performed from the 1970s to the end of the 1990s. However, the particularity of my practice lies in the very application of such deconstructive, reflexive, and ambiguous means and meanings to share a critical questioning of age(ing).[19] Thus, the following sections substantiate

---

19 | In line with my discussion on age ambiguity as a subversive strategy in Chapter II I use the terms deconstruction, reflexivity and ambiguity as

my Practice as Research inquiry into age criticality on stage by tracing four key strategies to critique age(ing) featured in the *Fountain* solos. These are:

- Sliding Through Time
- Embracing Disorientation
- Undoing Age Appropriateness
- Inviting the Audience into Ambiguity

Sliding through Time

One important 'age-ambiguation' strategy of *Performing Age(ing)* is about the perception of time. During the studio research of *Solo Partnering* it became clear that different possibilities of relating age(ing) to time was a reoccurring interest. In my creative practice, I explored age(ing) through subjective interpretations and imaginations of past and future, of history, or through questions of rhythm, timing, and simultaneity. Ultimately, time and the experience of sliding through time became a central theme in *The Fountain of Age*.

In *The Fountain of Age*, which premiered in 2015 in London, I dance an excerpt of a piece I made twelve years earlier and therefore embody my younger dancer self, which in turn embodies a then imagined man in his mid sixties, by the name of K. Müh.[20] Similar to all the characters I create on stage, K. Müh is the result of imagining what I would be, what I would do, if my life had been different and other decisions had been taken. When performing an excerpt of this

---

holding related but slightly different meanings. I use ambiguity to advert to how something appears (on stage) to have more than one meaning. With deconstruction (as well discussed in Chapter II) I refer to the analytical perspective behind the conscious creation of ambiguous images or narratives. I understand reflexivity, as discussed in Chapter III, as an ability or tool necessary and used for both.

20 | Müh' or Mühe in German signifies arduousness. The phonetics of *K. Müh* in German sound like the French existentialist author Camus.

particular age narrative twelve years after its premiere, *K. Müh* is still around 65, still older than my current chronological age but at the same time also my past. Shortly after the scene with *K. Müh* appears a female age imagination of mine, addressed as *Claudia*, who seems slightly younger than *K. Müh*, and who, as I report, met *K. Müh* in the past. "This belongs to *Claudia*, [...] She met *K. Müh* during this legendary concert of Julio Iglesias in Hamburg, probably some of you were there, yes, it was very special, very special. *Claudia* is an expert in chair dances and hand dances" (Performance script *Fountain of Age*). By weaving a connection between these two imaginations of (my) age(ing), I multiply my imaginary futures and let them interact. Furthermore, as the date of the Iglesias concert is not mentioned, and as Iglesias is an entertainer whose career spans several generations, a specific temporal context, an historical anchoring is insinuated yet left undefined. However, *The Fountain of Age* does not only transfer past pieces into an ambiguous present but future works as well. At the end of the opening scene, wearing a baroque dress, I turn to the audience and say: "This was a piece I haven't made yet. But if it would be it would probably be like some of the other pieces from the last twelve years, something about the ambiguity of age(ing) and the multiplicity of time – chronological time – body time – theatrical time – imaginary time" (Performance script *Fountain of Age*).

In some way this corresponds to age researcher Anne Basting's proposal of seeing the body "in temporal depth" (1998: 22). She uses Butoh dancer Kazuo Ohno as an example to acknowledge that especially in performance it is possible to "imagine and embody past and potential changes across time" as well as to play with forward and backward imaginings (Basting 1998: 141). I am in this sense stressing the temporal depth of my currently staged body and my choreographic making in *The Fountain of Age*, when I switch back and forth between my already realised and still planned performances around age(ing). The images of each scene inform the reading of the following scene, giving my present body-self more ambiguity, multiplicity, or, in the words of Basting, more depth. As Basting says: "To see the body in depth is literally to see time across space. It is to witness the event of aging, to anticipate the changes the body will produce and to remember changes already passed" (1998: 141).

The Fountain of Age, London (2015)

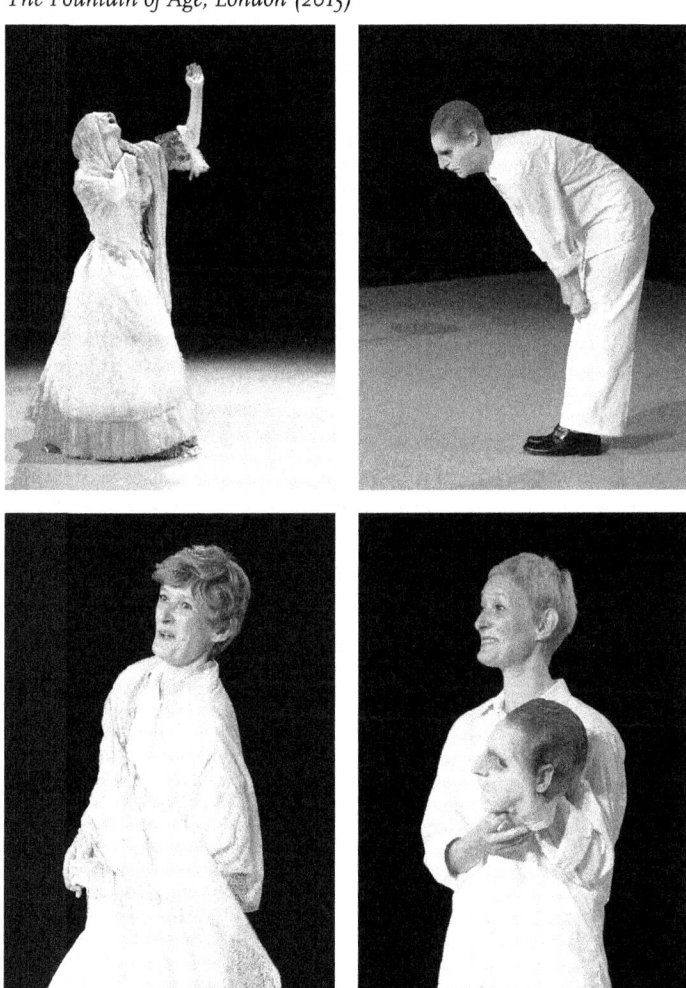

Photos: William Gillingham-Sutton

However, I would like to argue that *The Fountain of Age* departs from the linearity, or time-age-coherence suggested by Basting. Her reading of time across space or across the body remains within the logic of remembering the past (youth) and anticipating the future (old age). This fits how I read, for example, the performance *Forever Young* by Langkau and Waki, discussed earlier in this chapter. These performers look back at video footage from past artistic works (their youth), share their current aches, fears, and strategies of survival as midlife performers (their present) and imagine how they might continue their lives from now on (in the future) by creating an endless series of 'last performances'.

In contrast, and as my discussion above points out, *The Fountain of Age* operates in a different way. Notions of preview and retrospection overlap and contradict each other throughout the piece. I play with chronological age, with my own lifetime, and my possible age-selves in more complex ways and let the audience witness me sliding through time, transforming between different ages, genders, and times by changing movement material, masks, wigs, and temporal references. I suggest that such multilayered age and time narratives render the delineation between past, present and future permeable. Such sliding through time dissolves a coherent age narrative and thereby enables more intricate interpretations of age(ing) to gain visibility. What I call sliding through time is therefore a very specific age critical strategy, one that employs the principle of deconstruction as it directs the attention to what is "deemphasised" and "overlooked" (Balkin 1995-96:2) within dualistic notions of past and future and chronological age. It playfully questions the assumed inevitability of passing through time evenly and chronologically.

Embracing Disorientation

Another way in which Performing Age(ing) strengthens ambiguity instead of replicating ageist dualistic concepts, is to question the normative demand of being in control and autonomous. The scene *Improvisation & Dementia* in *The Fountain of Youth* (clip 1, min 11:00), for example, addresses disorientation as part of volatile processes of orientation.

Improvisation & Dementia in The Fountain of Youth, Gothenburg (2013)

Photo: Lars Åsling

I argue that this scene develops an affirmative narrative of disorientation at any age and therefore counters the dualistic concept of the healthy and therefore sovereign, coherent, and controlled young or midlife subject that later turns into a fragile, confused, old other.[21]

I keep thinking they have something going on – improvisation and dementia. Something like a friendship or a kinship. [...] Improvisation as never ending warm up, especially open solo improvisation. I warm up my orientation, my relations into the empty. Here, like so – and then, it's gone.

---

21 | Questions around the ideals and the limits of self-control, autonomy, and independence in relation to age(ing) as well as dementia are addressed for example by: Simon Biggs and Jason Powell (2001), Gullette (2014) Stephen G. Post (2014), and Lynne Segal (2014).

I connect and socialise here – now – like so. And then it's gone. I'm in a loop of constantly building my grounds, my basics, and when I stop doing it, it stops doing it. (Performance script *Fountain of Youth*)

This scene explores the idea of a kinship between solo improvisation and dementia through dancing and simultaneously speaking about the similarities between open solo improvisation and symptoms of dementia.[22] While I do not intend to misrepresent or undermine the suffering of people with dementia, I suggest that both states highlight immediacy and acutely deal with the question: What makes sense now? While dementia is an involuntary condition leading to a loss of spatial and temporal orientation as well as a decreasing ability to respond and make sense of the surrounding world,[23] an improviser enters voluntarily and with interest into a state of searching for orientation and ways of relating which were not set or rehearsed before and which can not be reused later. By indicating a relationship between dementia and solo improvisation, I question the distinction between them. Distinction, according to Bourdieu (1984), is one of the most important strategies to (re)produce norms, which in turn leads to exclusions as the established norm is the measurement for social recognition. Accordingly the scene on improvisation and dementia aims to evoke the sense of a blurred border between the social construction of an autonomous and productive youth and

---

22 | The National Health Service UK explains: "Dementia is a syndrome (a group of related symptoms) associated with an on going decline of the brain and its abilities. [...] According to the Alzheimer's Society there are around 800,000 people in the UK with dementia. One in three people over 65 will develop dementia, and two-thirds of people with dementia are women. The number of people with dementia is increasing because people are living longer. It is estimated that by 2021, the number of people with dementia in the UK will have increased to around 1 million" http://www.nhs.uk/conditions/dementia-guide/pages/about-dementia.aspx

23 | See for example: Dementia Collaborative Research Centres Australia, http://www.dementia-assessment.com.au/measures.html

midlife and that of a demented old age and thereby deconstructs this powerful distinction.

The decision to include dementia as a subject in my performance first originated in practicing *Solo Partnering* and the reoccurring challenge of finding and keeping focus and orientation during solo improvisation. When practicing solo improvisation I experience again and again a crisis of disorientation. I struggle to access the compositional knowledge, the improvisational curiosity, and the necessary mindfulness that helps to find purpose, focus, and orientation in improvised solo dancing.[24] Linking this to my discussion of improvisation at the end of Chapter II, I argue that disorientation is an integral part of improvisation and of a self, open to the unknown and to change. It is not something experienced practitioners eventually overcome, but it is one of the shifting constraints as well as potentials improvisation deals with. Smith (2003: 246-247), for example, calls the state of disorientation 'the gap',[25] whilst Novack (1990: 151) emphasises how disorientation, especially in contact improvisation, surfaces not only spatially but potentially socially and emotionally.

Another reason to involve the notion of dementia here is that it is gaining increasing attention in age(ing) discourses. The threatening prospect of losing one's mental capacity, control, and sense of self is prominently visible in current academic as well as popular media discussions on age(ing), health, demographic change, and

---

24 | In my practice documentation questions around searching for focus, concentration, orientation and memorising come up for example in my verbalising before and after dancing in *Walk & Talk* (clip 5), in the dialogue following the improvisation *Placing Body Parts in Space* (clip 6), as well as during and after *Private or Performance* (clip 11).

25 | The notion of gap lately inspired the special issue on contact improvisation *Framing the Gap: Contact [and] Improvisation* in the *Journal of Dance and Somatic Practices* edited by Misri Dey and Malaika Sarco-Thomas (2014).

systems of care.[26] Cultural age researcher Swinnen argues that these discourses conjure up an "Alzheimer Apocalypse" (2013: 12). Drawing on her argument, I contend that the discourse of fear around this age related illness contributes to establishing a threat scenario about the impending loss of one's sovereignty and autonomy. Such a threat, in turn, suggests that the self-controlled, sovereign, autonomous subject exists in the first place and is perceived as normal. This ostensible normality reinforces the demand on the individual to do everything to prevent or delay this loss.

As an artistic response, *Improvisation & Dementia* does not rehearse the concept of dance as a possible therapy to ward off the lingering threat of dementia. Instead, dance in my work functions as an affirmation of a constantly struggling, ever precarious bodymind that accepts disorientation to find orientation, which itself is only temporary. When I explicitly articulate the value and difficulty of embracing states and times of disorientation instead of enforcing hierarchical distinctions (Bourdieu 1984) and "dividing practices" (Foucault 1982: 777) in *Improvisation & Dementia* I implicitly gesture towards the idea that such dynamic subjectivity does not need to cast out the many different possible states of disorientation and infirmity that are associated with old age. This attitude is also resonant of Beauvoir's critique of casting out the old, an argument I used to open up my discussion of age studies in Chapter II. The question Beauvoir poses in *The Coming of Age* (1996) articulates the ethical dimension that underlies the age(ing) discourse in general as well as this research. She asks: What does "the meaning or the lack of meaning that old age takes on in any given society" reveal about that society as a whole? And what does it say about "the meaning or the lack of meaning of the entirety of the life leading to that old age" (Beauvoir 1996: 10)?

---

26 | See for example the discussions of dementia in the following journals: *Ageing & Society; Dementia – International Journal for Social Research and Practice; BMJ – The British Medical Journal*: http://www.bmj.com/specialties/dementia

Undoing Age Appropriateness

A further age critical strategy and explicit intervention into normative representations of age(ing) on stage is what I call 'undoing age appropriateness'. It is a strategy that resonates with Aggiss's claim for the "subversive expressive aging and fleshy body that exceeds expectations of what 'this' particular dancing body should be doing and where she should be doing it" (2014). It also relates to what Erica Stevens Abbitt et al. refer to as "older women who persist in making unruly spectacles of themselves" (2011: 50). *The Doc Martin Forever Young Meta Method* in *The Fountain of Youth* (clip 1, min 43:00) articulates the idea of undoing age appropriateness. As the scene plays out I present *The Doc Martin Forever Young Living Room Practice* as the first step of *The Doc Martin Forever Young Meta Method*, which I then demonstrate to the audience in the form of a four-minute dance to the James Bond signature tune. This dance, which concludes the "epic voyage towards the Fountain of Youth" (performance script), includes a mix of aerobic workout, free form improvisation and self-indulgent, erratic exploration of the stage, while at the same time getting drunk. As part of this living room practice I change into a flowery outfit chosen for its cheap exuberance. I also wear a grey wig so I seem more 'natural' and 'middle-age appropriate'. The proposed conclusion at the end of the journey in search of eternal youth is: "every movement is a movement", "search your cupboards, get into something fancy", "put on music that you really enjoy, don't judge, anything goes" (performance script *Fountain of Youth*). It is, simply put, accepting and using what is available, mixed with a willingness to play.

This rather simple proposal, however, is both ambiguous and painful. In the *Doc Martin Forever Young Living Room Practice* the playful freedom and self-acceptance of one's own body, movements, joys and preferences comes at a price in the form of a loss of dignity, conventionality and self-control. It is this very tension that the performance purposely leaves unsolved/unhealed. This unresolved place invokes the ambiguity of being both drawn to and embarrassed by a middle-aged woman who is tastelessly, ludicrously and joyously hopping around in an imaginary living room.

The Doc Martin Meta Method in The Fountain of Youth, Gothenburg (2013)

Photo: Lars Åsling

This is the last scene of this solo performance, and also the most parodic moment in the piece. More precisely, I parody myself, thus poking fun at my role as researcher and expert on age(ing) and as a midlife woman. Using such self-parodic representation of female midlife I seek to tease out the ambiguities in discriminating between appropriateness, ridiculousness, and dignity and thereby explore the borderlands of 'tastefulness'. As described in Chapter II, taste defines and is defined by a "sense of one's place" in the social world (Bourdieu 1984: 471). Bourdieu has shown how taste is an internalised aesthetic judgement anchored in and filled with normativity rather then being a purely individual preference. It operates, in consequence, as an expression and vehicle of social distinction and discrimination. When playing, for example, with a grey wig, ridiculous clothing, and dubious music my intention is to gently stretch the dominant sense of age related tastefulness.

The living room practice, therefore, challenges both my own and my audience's sense of social orientation by transgressing what is conventionally understood as a respectful and dignified representation of age(ing), or of being middle-aged. Or, borrowing from Butler (2004), the scene is an example of 'undoing age appropriateness'. I suggest the particular way of undoing age appropriateness in the living room practice therefore to be age critical. It aims to subvert the normative and gendered value of occupying a 'proper' place in the social world by appearing as young as possible and/or by replacing lost youthfulness with dignified behaviour and an appearance of seniority. The living room practice tries to show a paradox equal to that of the performance of gender norms, as explicated by Butler in *Undoing Gender*: "Indeed, the capacity to develop a critical relation to these norms presupposes a distance from them, and ability to suspend or defer a need for them, even as there is a desire for norms that might let one live" (2004: 3). Like Connell (1995), Butler claims that (gender) norms are not surrendered easily at all, because they are not merely unjust, restrictive chains to be broken but norms are also needed and desired since their structuring and regulating functions are also experienced as enabling and supportive in relation to some of our multiple social belongings. Butler continues: "The critical relation depends as well on a capacity, invariably collective, to articulate an alternative, minority version of sustaining norms or ideals that enable me to act" (2004: 3). Here Butler makes the important argument that the individual cannot fight or change norms defining and defined by the dominant agreements on taste and appropriateness, but needs to form a group or network to support one another in living according to other principles, thereby visibly installing alternative minority norms.

The theatrical situation, in this sense, allows me to perform an ostensibly individual and intimate 'first step' to transgress age norms, supposedly taking place inside a protecting private living room setting. The actual productive tension, however, derives from enacting the private practice in the hyper-exposed public situation of a theatre stage. This is important given that the transgression can only gain critical momentum and become a new 'minority norm' when it does not stay a hidden practice in the confines of the private living room, but instead is witnessed and considered by others, thereby possibly becoming a 'collective capacity'. That the audience witnesses the supposedly intimate living room practice is crucial for this playful undoing of age appropriateness. Accordingly, I argue that performance making enables a more explicitly age critical position, one that is heard and seen by an audience.

Inviting the Audience into Ambiguity

Deepening the discussion of the audience-performer relationship, this final section analyses how *Performing Age(ing)* attempts to make the theatre a hospitable site and a shared space for critical reflections on age(ing). In Chapter I I introduce the notion of hospitality as important for my performance making in general. In the context of *Performing Age(ing)* the notion of hospitality and building a situation of reciprocity or complicity has gained considerable significance. I consider creating an inviting, stimulating relationship as a strategy to encourage the audience to be open towards new, perhaps puzzling, complex and ambiguous perceptions of age(ing). I see the personal but clearly moderated and choreographed relationship created in *Performing Age(ing)* as a basic strategy to support the audience's entrance into an exploratory (re)consideration of age(ing) that playfully dares to go beyond the clichés and simplistic logic of the youth-age dualism.

Therefore, every time I speak in the piece I directly address the audience. Throughout the performances I maintain my basic attitude, namely that I am there as an individual offering my artistic wondering and pondering on age(ing) to the individuals who made the effort to come to this theatre. The general attitude of a host I inhabit also prepares the ground for moments of active audience participation, which are often part of *Performing Age(ing)*. In several works of *Performing Age(ing)* I have explored including the audience into my performances by giving them small tasks or roles to play that support the unfolding of the piece. Such participation invites complicity in the performance event, because the audience takes part in the simultaneous exposure and realisation of theatrical making. By such softening of the borders between performer and audience, between stage and auditorium, between watching and moving, I aim for a way of performing that the improviser and choreographer David Zambrano calls "sharing instead of showing" and "going on a journey together with the audience" (2011).[27]

To rephrase this in terms of a host-guest concept that tries to (re)consider age(ing), such participations invite the guests to actively take part in exploring and momentarily realising other imaginations and representations of age(ing). In *Performing Age(ing)* the audience takes part, for example, by embodying dedicated applauding fans asking for an encore, while I enact a dance diva whose best days are over (*Rosi tanzt Rosi* 2007). Or a dozen female audience members perform a multi-generational 'girls-line' for my old wannabe Casanova K. Müh (*K. Müh/JULIO* 2003-2006). Claudia offers the audience to develop their brave and daring sides by joining a kissing experiment (*Claudia/JULIO* 2004-2006).

---

27 | This quote is taken from my personal notes, made during my participation in Zambrano's workshop "Improvisation on Stage", Berlin, April 2011. For more information on Zambrano see his website: www.davidzambrano.org

From the left: Claudia in JULIO, Bassano di Grappa (2007); K. Müh in JULIO, Gothenburg (2008)

Photo: Antonella Travascio; video still: Niklas Rydén

IV. Performing Age(ing)   159

Unlike the activities around K. Müh and Claudia, the audience participation during *The Fountain of Youth* is not intended so that they empathise with an aged stage persona by taking part in his or her unfolding life story on stage. Instead, the participatory scene that I have named *Forever Young Exercises* is an invitation to a moment of playful communal testing and tasting of self-care practices related to youth and age. "One thing I did was looking for forever young exercises. The great thing about forever young exercises is that you can't be too young or too old to do them. So I thought I teach you now two exercises I liked in particular. Please stand up and join me on stage" (Performance script *Fountain of Youth*).

Forever Young Exercises in The Fountain of Youth, London (2014)

Video still: Dominique Rivoal

The two exercises that we explore together address the spine and work with spiralling. However, they are strikingly different in their conception, movement style, quality of concentration, as well as the sensations they generate. In this way I evade giving any trustworthy guideline or truth about what makes a good or 'rejuvenating' spine exercise. Instead I try to share my own ambivalence around self-care practices by means of the dissimilarity of the two exercises, as well as by my own attitude of testing myself still these exercises while instructing them, plus evoking a slightly comical effect by playing Bob Dylan's *Forever Young* as background music. In this way I try to offer the audience a space that allows for doubt and critical alertness while at the same time playfully engaging with the exercises offered.

Thus I suggest the dissolving of the border between performer and audience invites my guests to take part in 'dubious' practices and in amusing but not necessarily comfortable explorations around age(ing). The scene proposes what Haller calls an *"unentscheidbare Doppelwertigkeit"*, an indecidable ambivalence (my translation) (Haller 2011: 362).[28] Such deconstructive strategy, or strategic ambiguation of what might keep us 'young forever' tries to make the theatre a shared space for critical reflections on age(ing).

Summary

Through this chapter I have examined dance performances as moments in which artists can articulate and share with an audience an explicitly age critical position. I debate my concept of age critical performance making through examples from the current dance field and through an in-depth discussion of aspects of my own performance works. In the first part of this chapter my analysis of current performance practice has lead to the identification of three recurring strategies. I argue that they are pertinent approaches to developing age critical performance works and either make sense of age(ing) in terms of resisting the imperative of youthfulness, or reconcile with age(ing) and death, or stage more absurd, unresolved representations of age(ing) that collide with normative expectations and fears around age(ing).

As discussed in the second part of this chapter, my own performance practice *Performing Age(ing)* aims to complicate the question of how to think and deal with age(ing) even further by taking a decon-

---

28 | Haller's work on ambiguity and undoing age(ing) is discussed in Chapter II.

structive perspective on age(ing). *Performing Age(ing)* is presented as a long-term performance practice that aims at creating performances, which explore, apply, and aim to extend the idea of the age critical potential of dance by offering the audience a broader spectrum of concepts, images, narratives, or ways of dealing with age(ing). Based on *The Fountain of Youth* and *The Fountain of Age* I discuss four original age critical performance strategies that emerged in my Practice as Research. I first examine how my performance practice creates a sliding perception of time and age, one whose aim is to dissolve a coherent and chronology-based age narrative to enable more intricate interpretations of age(ing). The second strategy discussed is the affirmative narrative of disorientation at any age, which questions the normative demand of being in control and autonomous. Thirdly, the aim of my parodic representation of the 'middle-aged woman' is to intervene into normative representations of age(ing) by undoing age appropriateness. Finally, as my fourth original performance strategy I discuss how to invite the audience into ambiguous images and narratives that continuously open up the meaning of age(ing) towards multiplicity.

Conclusion

The research project *Dancing Age(ing)* examines contemporary dance in its potential to rethink age(ing) as well as its capacity to act as a site of practice for age criticality. The research principally asks: How can dance participate in a critical discourse on age(ing), and what new insights can my practice generate that inform the field of dance, and therefore contribute to the existing knowledge about such a critical engagement?

This inquiry has its roots in a range of prior pursuits. The first is a decade of creating performances that have addressed age(ing) coupled with a continuing curiosity about the subject. Secondly, I recognised that dedicated specialist practitioners of improvisation in their fifties and older share an approach to work and life that is continuously open to possibility and in contradiction to the culturally dominant age(ing) narratives. This realisation inspired me to explore this territory further. Thirdly, my research is rooted in my own lifelong involvement with dance improvisation, which is at times in the foreground, and at times in the background of my performance works. Finally, it is sparked by a conundrum I have been confronted with since my childhood and that I have heard with minor variation from many of my colleagues: Am I already too old to dance? These various strands together led to my interest to discover and make visible different potentials for rethinking age(ing). Thus this Practice as Research project investigates and creates original artistic practices that propose alternatives to the reiteration of the grand narratives of age(ing), such as the 'progress-peak-decline' narrative or the 'youthful nature of dance' and offer reflexive artistic interventions into the current age(ing) discourse.

Dancing Age(ing) builds on the idea of an age critical dance practice. It argues that improvisation practitioners in particular develop and employ ways of working that do age(ing) differently, and that have the potential to be identified as implicitly age critical. It further argues that performance is the site to represent age(ing) differently by way of articulating explicitly age critical narratives and images. These implicit and explicit aspects of contemporary dance making both contribute to developing such an age critical dance practice.

Within the frame of Practice as Research, the inquiry relies upon two original methods developed as part of the research process: *Solo Partnering* and performative interviewing. The first of these, *Solo Partnering*, is an improvisation practice remodelled from a method I generally use to train in solo improvisation. Here the approach was focused on becoming a creative, investigative method to find other associations, representations, and imaginations of/for age(ing). Further, methods of qualitative interviewing were remodelled to become a performative method that allows the participating expert practitioners to tap into their unique improvisation and performance expertise when addressing their particular understanding of age(ing). As such my methods stay intentionally close to artistic practice yet also become productive for Practice as Research. The development of such methods speaks to the potential and necessity of Practice as Research to work with idiosyncratic methods that draw from and speak to the particular research context, that are, as it were, custom built for a particular research project. Thus *Dancing Age(ing)* interweaves a variety of sources such as my own artistic research/practice, *Solo Partnering*, the voices of dancers with an outstanding expertise in improvisation, performance works that explicitly address age(ing), and strands of age theory.

Together these strands shape this mixed mode research articulated throughout this text and in the two solo performances, *The Fountain of Youth* and *The Fountain of* Age. Both performances continue and enhance my long-term performance practice called *Per-*

forming Age(ing). The role of the performances is central and stands on a par with the text as a research outcome. As complex artistic articulations of rethinking age(ing), the performances exceed the text and can be seen as new ways of knowing. The contribution of this work as a whole, therefore, is the expression of embodied and theoretically informed knowledge on age critical dance practice, which has not previously been articulated, composed, contextualised or staged in this way.

The central findings of *Dancing Age(ing)*, made possible through my particular Practice as Research approach, offer new angles to the discourses on dance and age(ing) and take part in rethinking the relationship between dance and age(ing) more generally. To begin with, I identify and position the discourses of age studies as pertinent for deepening our understanding of the relationship between dance and age(ing). Engaging with early age theorists such as Beauvoir (original text 1970) and Sontag (1972), as well as more recent ones, such as Haller (e.g. 2011) and Schwaiger (e.g. 2012), enabled me to underscore that our conceptions of age(ing) are culturally constructed in complex ways. Building on the existing critical analyses of age studies, I contend that the focus on youth embedded in the macrostructures of dance reflects more generally an established ageism. The idea of a natural decline of ability does not hold as reason for the traditionally short career of performing dancers in Western artistic dance. I argue that the dominant understanding of age(ing) in the dance profession naturalises a supposed youthfulness and reiterates an oversimplified progress-peak-decline narrative that glosses over underlying issues of debilitating power structures and the problems of a generally underfinanced professional field.

My inquiry into the discourses of age as well as dance studies further reveals some interesting gaps. On the one hand, the age critical discussion of dance incited by Schwaiger (2006, 2009, 2012) does not lead her to analyse the actual doings and details of experimental dance practices and existing performances, ones she highlights as promising for rethinking age(ing). On the other hand, scholarly writing that focuses on details of improvisation (as such an experimental practice) or on the critical potentials of contemporary performance making, such as Bormann, Brandstetter, Matzke (2010) and Husemann (2009) largely leave age(ing) unaddressed. *Dancing Age(ing)* fills such gaps by identifying and further developing a range of concrete age critical features in improvisation practices and in performance making, and it is to these findings that I now turn.

To investigate improvisation practice I offered some reflections on my own experiences. I also engaged with the practices and statements of Chung, Crisp, Eriksson, Hamilton, Morrish, and Simson, six dance artists for whom improvisation is the central artistic articulation and practice. It became clear that there were similarities in the way we all shape our practice and career, and each of the shared characteristics challenge the established youth-orientation in dance and constitute an implicitly critical position to dominant understandings of age(ing) in dance.

The first characteristic is the building of microstructure for sustained artistic practice, which allows improvisation focused artists to maintain and nourish an ongoing creative practice beyond early midlife. They create peer-supportive, and practice oriented modes of working that reflect the underlying concepts and principles of improvisation, such as prioritising time and space for creative inquiry and open-ended processes. These priorities stand in conflict to the competitive youth and news oriented funding in dance and how contemporary dance works are disseminated. Accordingly, these artists distance themselves from the arts market and follow a mixed mode strategy of artistic and economic survival at the margins of the current macrostructures of dance. Thus operating at a distance from the macrostructures of dance can be regarded as a mode of realising the improvising subject's relative agency and being less "governed" (Foucault 1997: 29) by detrimental age norms.

As a second shared characteristic all the abovementioned artists acknowledge and accept the existence of physical constraints. They are all engaged in multifaceted, explorative, and somatically informed care for and research into their individual dancing bodies. I argue that the particular ability to deal with and integrate physical constraints is again inherently connected to the core principles of improvisation, such as focussing on what is available here and now, ongoingness, and practicing an unstable self, open to possibility. Realising an open-ended personalised physical practice that can accommodate shifting physical constraints implies alternatives to oversimplifying and static notions of health and linear decline narratives critiqued in age theory.

Furthermore, by developing and discussing my research/practice *Solo Partnering*, I identify the cultivation of reflexive dialogues as a third characteristic of improvisation that can inform the rethinking of age(ing) in dance. Based on my research I contend that reflexivity is a basic underlying tool through which improvisation focused dance artists realise their specific ecology of long-term practice. Moreover, I argue that specific aspects of the reflexivity developed and trained in improvisation actually correspond with the objectives of age critique and, therefore, can prepare the ground and offer practical tools that enable an explicitly age critical practice. More precisely, refinement and differentiation in perception and action, trained in improvisation, might allow recognition and suspension of dualistic stereotypes of age(ing). Similarly, releasing one's presumptions and conventions might enable a recognition and suspension of one's own hidden or internalised ageism. To be sure, working with the possibilities of the here and now has the potential to interrupt the impulse of narrating age(ing) as decline or as 'wise' withdrawal.

The ways in which reflexivity in improvisation practice can be activated and used for creating an explicit age critique is contained in the research findings on my performance practice *Performing Age(ing)*. Accordingly, my findings in regard to the potential of performance for explicit age critique are discussed in Chapter IV. To contextualise the particular age critique developed in and through *Performing Age(ing)* I first identify explicitly age critical representations of age(ing) found in the statements and performances of currently active dance artists such as Aggiss, Crisp, Hay, Houstoun,

Langkau, Morrish, Rainer, Tompkins, and Waki. I determine three modes of how age(ing) is reconfigured in these artists' work in ways that complicate the grand narratives of age(ing). Some of the artists articulate a level of resistance against the pervasive focus on youth in dance, which I consider to be the first mode. Others lean towards a reconciliatory perspective on age(ing), which emphasises a sense of age(ing)'s meaningfulness and forms the second mode. A third group stresses the unresolvable collision between normative expectations on age(ing) and individual desire, which I identify as the third mode.

Performing Age(ing) develops yet another age critical mode that focuses on 'ambiguating' age(ing), thus it relates to and extends the theoretical discussions of age-ambiguity by Haller and Schwaiger. It builds on my reflexive improvisation practice and constitutes a gender reflective, deconstructive practice that emphasises contradictory and continuously changing perspectives and experiences, and ambiguous narratives and meanings of age(ing). In the *Fountain* pieces I explore how performance can make cultural conventions of age(ing) explicit and, in turn, can critically play with the scope of possibility and variation therein. The original age criticality the *Fountain* pieces have raised as research findings can be conceptualised by highlighting four strategies:

First, what I call *Sliding Through Time* is the strategic ambiguation of chronological time and static age identity. It dissolves a coherent age narrative and thereby enables more intricate interpretations of age(ing) to gain visibility.

Second, *Embracing Disorientation* questions the normative demand of being in control and autonomous. It affirms a constantly struggling, ever precarious bodymind that accepts disorientation to find orientation, which itself is always only temporary. Such a dynamic and unstable subjectivity does not need to cast out the many different possible states of disorientation and infirmity that are associated with old age. *Embracing Disorientation* thus questions hierarchical "distinctions" (Bourdieu 1984) and "dividing practices" (Foucault 1982: 777) and indirectly picks up on Beauvoir's ethical question about the meaning or the lack of meaning that old age takes on in society.

The third strategy, *Undoing Age Appropriateness*, focuses on the possibility of transgressing age norms by playfully stretching the conventional sense of age related tastefulness. As such it takes part in articulating "an alternative, minority version of sustaining norms or ideals" (Butler 2004:3) beyond the normative and gendered value of occupying a 'proper' place in the social world by appearing as young as possible and/or by replacing lost youthfulness with dignified behaviour and an appearance of seniority.

The fourth strategy, *Inviting the Audience into Ambiguity*, explores ways to make the theatre a hospitable site and a shared space for a deconstructive questioning of age(ing). Explicitly avoiding the repetition of dualistic images and imaginations and any fixed notion of truth, it offers the audience a space that allows for doubt and critical alertness and invites to playfully engage in the ambiguation and "undoing" (Haller 2010: 216) of age(ing).

Consequently, *Performing Age(ing)* clearly proposes that the age(ing) discourse is neither bound to a senior audience nor to exceptionally older dancers on stage. Instead it shows that age(ing) is a subject that can be reflected upon and explicitly addressed artistically by artists and audiences of any chronological age. With specific reference to *The Fountain of Youth* and *The Fountain of Age* as the two main stage works developed within the framework of this research, I argue that in my specific age critical articulation I neither observe age or old subjects from a distance, as a positivist researcher might, nor do I address my own age(ing) process autobiographically as many of the other artists discussed in this book have done. Instead I use the reflexive capacities I developed in my ongoing improvisation practice to keep changing perspective. And I present age(ing) and my own age(ing) self as processes of multiplicity and unfixed creative interaction within constantly changing possibilities and constraints. Hence, the *Fountain* pieces share a reflexive questioning of the meanings of age(ing) and emphasise the multiplicity of narratives resulting from this questioning. In both pieces I use my midlife body to perform ambiguous and shifting ages and introduce less stereotypical and more complex perceptions of age(ing). In this sense I position *The Fountain of Youth* and *The Fountain of Age* as a practical artistic effort to deconstruct ageist dualistic concepts of gendered age(ing) by performing age(ing) ambiguously.

In conclusion, the range of implicitly age critical practices developed in improvisation, and the range of explicitly age critical narratives and images possibly made visible in performance, both show how dance artists can practice and stage their bodies in open-ended negotiation with the temporality and challenges of dance, of life and an ageist (dance) culture. By doing so, they offer valuable and critical impulses to the age(ing) discourse in dance and beyond.

My focus on articulating the age critical potentials in one specific field of dance practice has encouraged me to continue to focus on a limited number of artists and practices. I hope that this study inspires others to consider the experiences and expertise of dancers working in other dance traditions. The strategies and categories developed in this book could function as a starting point for similar or opposing categories in the practices and performances of artists working within non-Western dance lineages and/or operating within other geopolitical contexts to reveal a diversity of cultural norms and attitudes to age(ing) in and through dance. Indeed, other areas of possible investigation that this study generates is the notable gap in research considering dancers who do not continue their dancing careers past midlife, or studies that illuminate some dancers' unique paths of life and careers through an age critical lens. Each of these could be worth pursuing in future projects and would flesh out understandings about the effects of different perceptions of age(ing) in dance. Moreover, the precarious financial conditions that characterise the field of professional artistic dance in general (Baumol, Jeffri, Throsby 2004; Dümcke 2008) need to be addressed, as these conditions frame dance as a field exclusively of and for the latest generation.

As individualised strategies for sustaining one's practice are extremely volatile and limited in their scope there is a need to rethink the macrostructures of dance, and encourage an active societal interest in dance as an art form that covers the full spectrum of age. It would imply creating, as a consequence, new support structures for dance that encompasses all ages. However, my main point is not to argue for diversity and inclusion, but to acknowledge and further dance's potential as a creative, reflexive and somatically intelligent embodied practice that can influence how we conceptualise age(ing) more generally. To move such debates forward, existing practices, such as those explored in this study, could be given more attention and practically strengthened through rethinking existing arts funding systems. A concept like an unconditional basic income could be considered in its potential to support artist's long-term artistic development instead of reiterating "dividing practices" (Foucault 1982: 777) and entrepreneurial competition, which continuously perpetuate the production of "art-to-be" (Kunst 2012b) and "deprivation of time" (Kunst 2012a).

Thus *Dancing Age(ing)* raises many questions that point to avenues for further investigation. My research findings could inspire further age critical inquiry and the development of other specific age critical perspectives in the fields of improvisation and performance making. They could be taken up in the field of age theory as well as in those fields I left unaddressed, such as community dance, dance medicine, or gerontology research. It could also be exciting to see research into how the rethinking of age(ing) in and through dance I propose here could inspire the discourses and practices of dance education. In addition to these possibilities concerning research and policies, I personally look forward to continue developing performances that make the theatre a shared space for playful and critical reflections on age(ing). My formal and informal contacts with audiences in and around *Performing Age(ing)* confirm for me the unique potential of theatre to spark individual imagination as well as inspired dialogues with leeway for multiplicities of meanings, sheltered vertigo, productive misunderstandings, and inspiring awkwardness. Thus I am curious to see how this might contribute to moving our rethinking of age(ing) forward.

Works Cited

Abbitt, E. S., Frank, J., Harris, G. G., Mock, R. (2011) Aging Provocateurs and Spect(er)acular Pub(l)ic Performances. *Performance Research*, 16 (2), pp. 50-56.

Addison, H. (2010) "That Younger, Fresher Women": Old Wives for New (1918) and Hollywood's Cult of Youth. In: Lipscomb, V. B. and Marshall, L. (eds.) *Staging Age: The Performance of Age in Theatre, Dance, and Film*. New York: Palgrave Macmillan. pp. 11-26.

Aggiss, L. (2014a) *The English Channel*. Performance. Information retrieved at: http://www.lizaggiss.com/current/english-channel/ [Accessed 14 September 2015].

Aggiss, L. (2014b) *University of Brighton, Academic Staff: Aggiss*. [online]. Available from: http://arts.brighton.ac.uk/staff/liz-aggiss [Accessed 20 February 2014].

Aggiss, L. (2015) website. Available from: http://www.lizaggiss.com/ [Accessed 7 September 2015].

Ageing & Society. Journal. Cambridge: Cambridge University Press.

Albright, A. C. (1997) *Choreographing Difference: The Body and Identity in Contemporary Dance*. Middletown: Wesleyan University Press.

Albright, A. C. (2003a) Dwelling in Possibility. In: Albright, A. C. and Gere, D. (eds.) *Taken by Surprise: A Dance Improvisation Reader*. Middletown: Wesleyan University Press. pp. 257-266.

Albright, A. C. (2003b) Present Tense. In: Albright, A. C. and Gere, D. (eds.) *Taken by Surprise: A Dance Improvisation Reader*. Middletown: Wesleyan University Press. pp. 205-211.

Albright, A. C. and Gere, D. (eds.) (2003) *Taken by Surprise: A Dance Improvisation Reader*. Middletown: Wesleyan University Press.

Albright, A. C. (2011) Situated Dancing: Notes from Tree Decades in Contact with Phenomenology. *Dance Research Journal* 43 (2), pp. 7-18.

Alzheimer's Society (2013) website. Available from: http://www.alzheimers.org.uk/infographic [Accessed 1 September 2013].

Amans, D. (2008) Community Dance – What's That? In: Amans D. (ed.) *An Introduction into Community Dance Practice*. Basingstoke: Palgrave Macmillan. pp. 3-10

Aragonès, M. (2012) *Solo Partnering*. [e-mail correspondence with author, 2 August 2012].

Aragones, M. (2015) website. Available from: http://mireiaaragones.wix.com/consciousmovement# [Accessed 7 September 2015].

Bacon, J. and Midgelow, V. (2010) Articulating Choreographic Practices, Locating the Field: An Introduction. *Choreographic Practices* 1, pp. 3-19.

Balkin, J. M. (1995-96) *Deconstruction* [online]. Available from: http://www.yale.edu/lawweb/jbalkin/articles/deconessay.pdf [Accessed 20 April 2015].

Banes, S. (1987) *Terpsichore in Sneakers: Post-Modern Dance*. Middletown: Wesleyan University Press.

Banes, S. (1995) *Democracy's Body: Judson Dance Theatre, 1962 – 1964*. Durham: Duke University Press.

Banes, S. (1998) *Dancing Women: Female Bodies on Stage*. New York: Routledge.

Barrett, E. and Bolt, B. (eds.) (2007) *Practice as Research: Approaches to creative arts inquiry*. London: I. B. Tauris.

Baumol, J. W., Jeffri, J., Throsby, D. (2004) *Making Changes: Facilitating the Transition of Dancers to Post-Performance Careers. Research Project*. [online]. Available from: http://www.cpanda.org/data/a00191/changes.pdf [Accessed 2 January 2013].

Beauvoir, S. de (1996) *The Coming of Age*. (O'Brian, P. trans). New York: Norton. Originally published as La Veillesse (1970) Paris: Gallimard.

Benjamin, A. (2010) Cabbages and Kings: Disability, Dance, and some Timely Considerations. In: Carter, A. and O'Shea, J. (eds.) *The Routledge Dance Studies Reader.* London: Routledge. pp. 111-121.

Benoit-Nader, A. (ed.) (1997) On the Edge/Créateurs de l'Imprévu. *Nouvelles de Danse 32/33.* Brussels: Contredanse.

Berson, J. (2010) Old Dogs, New Tricks: Intergenerational Dance. In: Lipscomb, V. B. and Marshall, L. (eds.) *Staging Age: The Performance of Age in Theatre, Dance, and Film.* New York: Palgrave Macmillan. pp. 165-189.

Biggs, S. and Powell, J. L. (2001) A Foucauldian Analysis of Old Age and the Power of Social Welfare. *Journal of Ageing and Social Policy* 12 (2), pp. 93-112.

BMJ: The British Medical Journal (2015) *Dementia from BMJ.* [online]. Available from: http://www.bmj.com/specialties/dementia [Accessed 7 September 2015].

Bolton, G. (2010) *Reflective Practice: Writing and Professional Development.* Third Edition. Thousand Oaks: Sage.

Borgdorff, H. (2007) *Artistic Research Within the Fields of Science.* [online]. Available from: http://www.gu.se/digitalAssets/1322/1322679_artistic-research-within-the-fields-of-science.pdf [Accessed 2 July 2011].

Bormann, H. F., Brandstetter, G., Matzke, A. (eds.) (2010) *Improvisieren: Paradoxien des Unvorhersehbaren.* Bielefeld: Transcript.

Bourdieu, P. (1984) *Distinction: A Social Critique of the Judgment of Taste.* (Nice, R. trans.) Cambridge: Harvard University Press. Originally published as *La Distinction: Critique Sociale du Jugement* (1979) Paris: Les Éditions de Minuit.

Braidotti, R. (1994) Nomadic Subjects: Embodiment and Sexual Difference in Contemporary Feminist Theory. New York: Columbia University Press.

Braidotti, R. (2006a) Affirming the Affirmative: On Nomadic Affectivity. *Rhizomes* 11/12. [online]. Available from: http://www.rhizomes.net/issue11/ [Accessed 18 October 2014].

Braidotti, R. (2006b) Affirmation versus Vulnerability: On Contemporary Ethical Debates. *Symposium* 10 (1). pp. 235-254.

Brayshaw, T. and Witts, N. (2014) *The Twentieth-Century Performance Reader*. Third Edition. Abingdon: Routledge.

Brecht, B. (1963) *Schriften zum Theater 5: Der Messingkauf/Übungsstücke für Schauspieler/Gedichte aus dem Messingkauf*. Frankfurt: Surkamp.

Bremser, M. and Sanders, L. (eds.) (2011) *50 Contemporary Choreographers*. Abingdon: Routledge.

Brunette, P. and Wills, D. (1994) The Spatial Arts: An Interview with Jacques Derrida. In: Brunette, P. and Wills, D. (eds.) *Deconstruction and the Visual Arts: Art, Media, Architecture*. Cambridge: Cambridge University Press. pp. 9-32.

Buckwalter, M. (2010) *Composing While Dancing: An Improvisers Companion*. Wisconsin: University of Wisconsin Press.

Burns, L. (2014) The English Channel. *Exeunt*. [online]. Available from: http://exeuntmagazine.com/reviews/the-english-channel/ [Accessed 14 September 2015].

Burrows, J. and Fargio, M. (2014) *The Elders Project*. Performance. [online]. Available from: http://rescen.net/blog_elix/?p=509 [Accessed 28 September 2014].

Burt, R. (1995) *The Male Dancer: Bodies, Spectacle, Sexualities*. Abingdon: Routledge.

Burt, R. (2006) *Judson Dance Theatre: Performative Traces*. Abingdon: Routledge.

Butler, J. (1988) Performance Acts and Gender Constitution: An Essay in Phenomenology and Feminist Theory. *Theatre Journal* 40 (4), pp. 519-531.

Butler, J. (1993) *Bodies That Matter: On the Discursive Limits of Sex*. New York: Routledge.

Butler, J. (2001) *What is Critique? An Essay on Foucault's Virtue*. [online]. Available from: http://eipcp.net/transversal/0806/butler/en [Accessed 14 November 2014].

Butler, J. (2004) *Undoing Gender*. New York: Routledge.

Butler, R. N. (1969) Age-ism: Another Form of Bigotry. *Gerontologist* 9 (4), pp. 243-246.

Carter, A. (1996) Bodies of Knowledge: Dance and Feminist Analysis. In: Campell P. (ed.) *Analysing Performance: A Critical Reader*. Manchester: Manchester University Press. pp. 43-55.

Charmaz, K. (2006) *Constructing Grounded Theory: A Practical Guide through Qualitative Analysis*. Thousand Oaks: Sage.

Chung, R. (2011) Interview with Author. [online]. Available from: https://vimeo.com/album/3144399/video/120157511 [Accessed 17 October 2016].

Chung, R. (2013) website. Available from: http://www.italycontactfest.com/insegnanti-2013/ray-chung/ [Accessed 3 February 2013].

Chung, R., Eriksson, K., Martin, S. (2014) *Artistic Response to Age(ing)*. [online]. Available from: https://vimeo.com/album/3144399/video/115800922 [Accessed 17 October 2016].

Claid, E. (2006) *Yes? No! Maybe...: Seductive Ambiguity in Dance*. Abingdon: Routledge.

Coghlan, D. and Brannick, T. (2010) *Doing Action Research in Your Own Organization*. Thousand Oaks: Sage.

Connell, R. (1995) *Masculinities*. Cambridge: Polity Press.

Connolly, M. K. and Redding, E. (2010) *Dancing Towards Well-Being in the Third Age*. [online]. Available from: http://www.trinitylaban.ac.uk/media/315435/literature%20review%20impact%20of%20dance%20elderly%20populations%20final%20draft%20with%20ologos.pdf [Accessed 20 October 2013].

Cooney, S. (2012) *Solo Partnering*. [e-mail correspondence with author, 29 June 2012].

Cooney, S. (2015) website. Available from: http://www.shannoncooney.org/ [Accessed 7 September 2015].

Crisp, R. (2012) *Artistic Response to Age(ing)*. [online]. Available from: https://vimeo.com/album/3144399/video/115746066. [Accessed 17 October 2016].

Crisp, R. (2015) website. Available from: http://www.omeodance.com/ [Accessed 7 September 2015].

Csikszentmihalyi, M. (1990) *Flow: The Psychology of Optimal Experience*. New York: Harper and Row.

Dance On (2016) website. Available from: http://dance-on.net/en/ [Accessed 15 October 2016].

Debus, K., Könnecke, B., Schwerma, K., Stuve, O. (eds.) (2012) *Geschlechterreflektierte Arbeit mit Jungen an der Schule.* Berlin: Dissens e.V. [online]. Available from: http://www.jungenarbeit-und-schule.de/fileadmin/Redaktion/Dokumente/Buch/Geschlechter-reflektierte_Arbeit_mit_Jungen_an_der_Schule_Dissens_e.V-3.pdf [Accessed 30 August 2015]

Dementia Collaborative Research Centre Australia Dementia Assessment (2013) website. Available from: http://www.dementia-assessment.com.au/measures.html [Accessed 1 September 2013].

Dementia: The International Journal for Social Research and Practice. Journal. Thousand Oaks: Sage.

Denzin, N. K. (2014) *Interpretive Autoethnography.* Second Edition. Thousand Oaks: Sage.

Derrida, J. (1982) Signature, Event, Context. In: Derrida, J. *Margins of Philosophy.* (Bass, A. trans.), Chicago: University of Chicago Press. pp. 307-329. Originally published as *Marges de la Philosophie* (1972) Paris: Les Éditions de Minuit.

Desmond, J.C. (ed.) (2001) *Dancing Desire: Choreographing Sexualities On and Off the Stage.* Madison: University of Wisconsin Press.

De Spain, K. (2003) The Cutting Edge of Awareness: Reports from the Inside of Improvisation. In: Albright, A. C. and Gere, D. (eds.) *Taken by Surprise.* Middletown: Wesleyan University Press. pp. 27-38.

De Spain, K. (1997) *Solo Movement Improvisation: Constructing Understanding through Lived Somatic Experience.* Unpublished PhD thesis. Temple University.

De Spain, K. (2014) *Landscape of the Now: A Topography of Movement Improvisation.* New York: Oxford University Press.

Dey, M. and Sarco-Thomas, M. (2014) (eds.) Framing the Gap: Contact [and] Improvisation. *Journal of Dance and Somatic Practices* 6 (2).

Dickinson, B. (2010) Age and the Dance Artist. In: Lipscomb, V. B. and Marshall, L. (eds.) *Staging Age: The Performance of Age in Theatre, Dance, and Film.* New York: Palgrave Macmillan. pp. 191-206.

Diemer, H. (1990) *Lesgeven in Dansexpressie.* Rotterdam: Rotterdamse Dansacademie.

Duck, K. (2015) website. Available from: http://katieduck.com/ [Accessed 7 September 2015].

Dümcke C. (2008). *Transition Zentrum Tanz in Deutschland (TZTD), Projektstudie zur Modellentwicklung.* [online]. Available from: http://www.cultureconcepts.de/files/Transition%20Tanz%20D%20Studie_Lang_02_2008.pdf [Accessed 5 August 2012].

Eriksson, K. (2011) Interview with Author. [online]. Available from: https://vimeo.com/album/3144399/video/119118847. [Accessed 17 October 2016].

Eriksson, K. (2015) website. Available from: https://plus.google.com/+KatarinaErikssonIMPRO/about [Accessed 7 September 2015].

Faircloth C. A. (2003) *Aging Bodies: Images and Everyday Experience.* Walnut Creek: Altamira.

Featherstone, M. (1991) The body in consumer culture. In: Featherstone M., Hepworth M., Turner B. S. (eds.) *The Body: Social Process and Cultural Theory.* Thousand Oaks: Sage.

Fensham, R. (2013) "Breakin' the Rules": Elo Pomare and the Transcultural Choreographies of Black Modernity. *Dance Research Journal* 45 (1), pp. 41-63.

Fiadero, J. (2015) website. Available from: http://www.re-al.org/en/companhia-re-al/ [Accessed 7 September 2015].

Foster, S. L. (1986) *Reading Dancing: Bodies and Subjects in Contemporary American Dance.* Berkeley: University of California Press.

Foster, S. L. (1997) Dancing Bodies. In: Desmond, J. C. (ed.) *Meaning in Motion.* Durham: Duke University Press. pp. 235-257.

Foster, S. l. (2002) *Dances That Describe Themselves: The Improvised Choreography of Richard Bull.* Middletown: Wesleyan University Press.

Foster, S. L. (2009) (ed.) *Worlding Dance.* New York: Palgrave Macmillan.

Foster, S. (2010) Dancing Bodies: Ad Addendum, 2009. *Theater* 40 (1), pp. 25-29.

Foucault, M. (1982) The Subject and Power. *Critical Inquiry* 8 (4), pp. 777-795.

Foucault, M. (1984) *Foucault*. [online]. Available from: http://foucault.info/foucault/biography.html [Accessed 12. July 2015].

Foucault, M. (1995) *Discipline and Punish: The Birth of the Prison*. (Sheridan, A. M. trans.) New York: Vintage. Originally published as *Surveiller et punir*. (1975) Paris: Éditions Gallimard.

Foucault, M. (2003) *The Birth of the Clinic: An Archeology of Medical Perception*. (Sheridan, A. M. trans) Abingdon: Routledge. Originally published as *Naissance de la Clinique* (1963) Paris: Universitaires des France.

Foucault, M. (2005) The Hermeneutics of the Subject: Course Summary. In: *The Hermeneutics of the Subject: Lectures at the College de France in 1981/82*. (Burchell, G. trans.) New York: Palgrave Macmillan. pp. 491-505. Originally published as *Herméneutique du Sujet*. (2001) Paris: Gallimard.

Foucault, M. (2007) What is Critique? In: Lotringer, S. (ed.) *The Politics of Truth*. (Hochroth, L. trans) Los Angeles: Semiotext(e). pp. 41-81. Originally published as Qu' est-ce que la Critique? (1990) *Bulletin de la Société Française de la Philosophie* 84 (2), pp. 35-63.

Fraleigh, S. and Hanstein, P. (eds.) (1999) *Researching Dance: Evolving Modes of Enquiry*. London: Dance Books.

Franko, M. (2011) The Dancing Gaze Across Cultures: Kazuo Ohno's Admiring La Argentina. *Dance Chronicle* 34 (1), pp. 106-131.

Franko, M. (2012) *Martha Graham in Life and War: The Life in The Work*. New York: Oxford University Press.

Friedan, B. (1994) *The Fountain of Age*. New York: Simon & Schuster.

Freeman, J. (2010) *Blood Sweat and Theory: Research through Practice in Performance*. Oxford: Libri.

Gilligan, C. (1982) *In a Different Voice*. Cambridge: Harvard University Press.

Goldman, D. (2010) *I Want to be Ready: Improvised Dance as a Practice of Freedom*. Ann Arbor: University of Michigan Press.

Gubrium, J. F. and Holstein, J. A. (eds.) (2001) *Handbook of Interview Research: Context & Method.* Thousand Oaks: Sage.

Gullette, M. M. (1988) *Safe at Last in the Middle Years: The Invention of Midlife Progress Novel.* Berkeley: University of California Press.

Gullette, M. M. (1997) *Declining to Decline: Cultural Combat and the Politics of the Midlife.* Charlottesville: University of Virginia Press.

Gullette, M. M. (2004) *Aged By Culture.* Chicago: University of Chicago Press.

Gullette, M. M. (2011) *Agewise: Fighting the New Ageism in America.* Chicago: University of Chicago Press.

Gullette, M. M. (2014) Euthanasia as a Caregiving Fantasy in the Era of the New Longevity. *Age Culture Humanities* 1. [online]. Available from: http://ageculturehumanities.org/WP/issue-1/ [Accessed 12. December 2014].

Hall, S. (1996) The West and the Rest: Discourse and Power. In: Hall, S., Held, D., Hubert, D., and Thompson, K. (eds.) *Modernity.* Cambridge: Blackwell. pp. 184-227.

Haller, M. (2009) *Aging trouble: Aging Studies und die Diskursive Neubestimmung des Alter(n)s.* [online]. Available from: http://www.gwi-boell.de/sites/default/files/assets/gwi-boell.de/images/downloads/LadiesLunch30_Thesen_Haller_20032009.pdf [Accessed 20 October 2013].

Haller, M. (2010a) Aging Studies und Cultural Studies: Inter und Transdisziplinarität in Kulturwissenschaftlichen Alternsstudien. In: Breinbauer, I., Ferring, D., Haller, M., Meyer-Wolters, H. (eds.) *Transdisziplinäre Alter(n)sstudien: Gegenstände und Methoden.* Würzburg: Königshausen & Neumann. pp. 231-256.

Haller, M. (2010b) Undoing Age: Die Performativität des Alternden Körpers im Autobiographischen Text. In: Mehlmann, S. and Ruby, S. (eds.) *Für Dein Alter Siehst Du Aber Gut Aus: Von der Unsichtbarkeit des Alternden Körpers im Horizont des Demphraphischen Wandels.* Bielefeld: Transcript. pp. 215-233.

Haller, M. (2011) Dekonstruktion der „Ambivalenz": Poststrukturalistische Neueinschreibungen des Konzepts der Ambivalenz aus

Bildungstheoretischer Perspektive. *Forum der Psychoanalyse* 27, pp. 359-371.

Haller, M. (2013) Ambivalente Subjektivationen: Performativitätstheoretische Perspektiven auf die Transformation von Alters- und Geschlechternormen im Geronto-Feministischen Diskurs. In: Haller, M., Meyer-Wolters, H., Schulz-Nieswandt, F. (eds.) *Alterswelt und Institutionelle Strukturen*. Würzburg: Königshausen & Neumann. pp. 19-36.

Halprin, A. (2000) *Intensive Care: Reflections on Death and Dying*. Performance. Information retrieved from: https://annahalprindigitalarchive.omeka.net/exhibits/show/performances/intensivecare--reflections-on [Accessed 14 September 2015].

Hamilton, J. (2011) Interview with Author. [online]. Available from: https://vimeo.com/album/3144399/video/118338803. [Accessed 17 October 2016].

Hamilton, J. (2015) website. Available from: http://www.julyenhamilton.com/index.html [Accessed 7 September 2015].

Hartong, C. (1985) *Danskunst: Inleiding tot het Wezen en de Practijk van de Dans*. Amsterdam: Nederlands Instituut voor de Dans.

Hay, D. (2015) website. Available from: http://www.deborahhay.com [Accessed 7 September 2015].

Hechler, A. and Stuve, O. (2015) Weder ‚Normal' noch ‚Richtig'. Geschlechterreflektierte Pädagogik als Grundlage einer Neonazismusprävention: In: Hechler, A. and Stuve, O. (eds.) *Geschlechterreflektierte Pädagogik Gegen Rechts*. Leverkusen: Barbara Budrich. pp. 44-72.

Hetz, A. (2015) website. Available from: http://www.amoshetz.com/ [Accessed 7 September 2015].

Hoghe, R. (2005) Den Körper in den Kampf Werfen. In: Klein, G. and Sting, W. (eds.) *Performance: Positionen zur Zeitgenössischen Szenischen Kunst*. Bielefeld: Transcript. pp. 51-57.

Houston, S. (2005a) Dance for Older People. *Primary Health Care* 15 (8), pp. 18-19.

Houston, S. (2005b) Participation in Community Dance: a Road to Empowerment and Transformation? *New Theatre Quarterly* 21 (2), pp. 166-177.

Houston, S. (2005c) Dancing for Youthfulness. *Working for Older People* 9 (2), pp. 15-17.

Houston, S. (2011) The Methodological Challenges of Researching Dance for People living with Parkinson's. *Dance Research* 29 (2), pp. 329-351.

Houstoun, W. (2011) *50 Acts*. Performance.[Nottingham: Nottingham Contemporary, 4 March 2011].

Houstoun, W. (2013) *Performance Project 'Making it up'*. [online]. Available from: http://www.independentdance.co.uk/author/wendy-houstoun/ [Accessed 10 October 2013].

Houstoun, W. (2014) *Pact with Pointlessness*. Performance. [Information retrieved from: http://www.wendyhoustoun.net/#!pact-with-pointlessness/c1tiv Accessed 14 September 2015].

Houston, W. (2015) website. Available from: http://www.wendyhoustoun.net/ [Accessed 7 September 2015].

Hutcheon, L. (1985) *A Theory of Parody: The Teachings of Twentieth-Century Art Forms*. New York: Methuen.

Hutmacher, E. (2015) website. Available from: http://www.alte-feuerwache.de/academy/t/inside/dozenten.php [Accessed 7 September 2015].

Husemann, P. (2009) *Tanz als Kritische Praxis: Arbeitsweisen bei Xavier Le Roy und Thomas Lehmen*. Bielefeld: Transcript.

Improvisation Xchange Berlin (2016) website. Available from: http://www.berlinartsunited.com/festival/ [Accessed 7 September 2016].

International Association for Dance Medicine and Science (2013) website. Available from: http://www.iadms.org/ [Accessed: 1 September 2013].

International Contact Festival Freiburg (2015) website. Available from: http://www.contactfestival.de/english/festival/festival.htm [Accessed: 8 September 2015].

Jowitt, D. (2011) Introduction. In: Bremser, M. and Sanders, L. (eds.) *50 Contemporary Choreographers*. Second Edition. Abingdon: Routledge. pp. 1-17.

Jürs-Munby, K. (2006) Introduction. In: Lehmann, H.T. *Postdramatic Theatre* (Jürs-Munby, K. trans.) Abingdon: Routledge. pp. 1-15.

Kaplan, E. A. (2010) The Unconscious of Age: Performances in Psychoanalysis, Film, and Popular Culture. In: Lipscomb, V. B. and Marshall, L. (eds.) *Staging Age: The Performance of Age in Theatre, Dance, and Film*. New York: Palgrave Macmillan. pp. 11-26.

Kask, E. (ed.) (2012) *About Improvisation*. Viljandi: Evestuudio.

Kattenstroth, J. C., Kalisch, T., Kolankowska, I., and Dinse, H. R. (2011) Balance, Sensorimotor, and Cognitive Performance in Long-Year Expert Senior Ballroom Dancers. *Journal of Aging Research* 2011 [online]. Available from: http://www.neuralplasticitylab.de/index.aspx?resort=4 [Accessed 30 July 2015].

Kattenstroth, J.- C., Kalisch, T., Holt, S., Tegenthoff, M., Dinse, H. R. (2013) Six Months of Dance Intervention Enhances Postural, Sensorimotor, and Cognitive Performance in Elderly Without Affecting Cardio-Respiratory Functions. *Frontiers in Aging Neuroscience* 5 [online]. Available from: http://www.neuralplasticitylab.de/index.aspx?resort=4 [Accessed 30 July 2015].

Keiz, A. (2012) *Solo Partnering*. [e-mail correspondence with author, 29 July 2012].

Keiz, A. (2015) website. Available from: https://vimeo.com/user4886549/videos/all [Accessed 7 September 2015].

Kemmis, S., Wilkinson, J., Edwards-Groves, C., Hardy, I., Grootenboer, P., Bristol, L. (2014) *Changing Practices, Changing Education*. Singapore: Springer.

Kershaw, B. and Nicholson, H. (eds.) (2011) *Research Methods in Theatre and Performance*. Edinburgh: Edinburgh University Press.

Kießling, B. (2012) *Solo Partnering*. [e-mail correspondence with author, 22 July 2012].

Kießling, B. (2015) website. Available from: https://brigittekiessling.wordpress.com/ [Accessed 7 September 2015].

Klein, G. (2013) Dance Theory as a Practice of Critique. In: Brandstetter, G. and Klein, G. (eds.) *Dance [and] Theory*. Bielefeld: transcript. pp. 137-149.

Kolb, A. (2009) *Performing Femininity: Dance and Literature in German Modernism*. Bern: Peter Lang.

Koteen, D. and Stark Smith, N. (2008) *Caught Falling: The Confluence of Contact Improvisation*. Northampton: Contact Editions.

Kriebernegg, U. and Maierhofer. R. (eds.) (2013) *The Ages of Life: Living and Aging in Conflict*. Bielefeld: Transcript.

Kunst, B. (2009) The Economy of Proximity. Dramaturgical Work in Contemporary Dance. *Performance Research* 14 (3), pp. 81-88.

Kunst, B. (2012a) The Project Horizon: On the Temporality of Making. *Manifesta* 16 [online]. Available from: http://www.manifestajournal.org/issues/regret-and-other-back-pages/project-horizon-temporality-making [Accessed 1 July 2013].

Kunst, B. (2012b) *The Project Horizon: On the Temporality of Art Making*. Lecture abstract [online]. Available from: http://www.uferstudios.com/veranstaltungen/alle-veranstaltungen/event/325 [Accessed: 12 July 2012].

Kunst, B. (2012c) Art and Labour: On Consumption, Laziness and Less Work. *Performance Research* 17 (6), pp. 116-125.

Lampert, F. (2007) *Tanzimprovisation: Geschichte – Theorie – Verfahren – Vermittlung*. Bielefeld: Transcript.

Landgraf, E. (2011) *Improvisation as Art: Conceptual Challenges, Historical Perspectives*. New York: Bloomsbury.

Langkau, T and Waki, Y. (2004/2011) *Schwund/Forever Young*. Performance [Berlin: Volksbühne 2004].

Lansley, J. and Early, F. (eds.) (2011) *The Wise Body: Conversations with Experienced Dancers*. Chicago: The University of Chicago Press.

Ledger, A. J., Ellis S., Wright F. (2011) The Question of Documentation: Creative Strategies in Performance Research. In: Kershaw, B. and Nicholson, H. (eds.) *Research Methods in Theatre and Performance*. Edinburgh: Edinburgh University Press. pp. 162-184.

Lehmann, H. T. (2006) *Postdramatic Theatre*. (Jürs-Munby, K. trans.) Abingdon: Routledge.

Levine, M. N. (2005) *Beyond Performance: Building a Better Future for Dancers and the Art of Dance.* [online]. Available from: http://www.iotpd.org/upl/advocacy-report-beyond-performance-pdf.pdf [Accessed: 12 December 2012].

Levy, B. R. and Banaji, M. R. (2002) Implicit Ageism. In: Nelson, T.D. (ed.) *Ageism: Stereotyping and Prejudice against Older Persons.* Cambridge: MIT Press. pp. 49-75.

Linsel, A. and Hoffmann, R. (2009) *Tanzträume: Jugendliche Tanzen Kontakthof von Pina Bausch.* Film. Köln: Real Fiction.

Lipscomb, V.B. and Marshall, L. (eds.) *Staging Age: The Performance of Age in Theatre, Dance, and Film.* New York: Palgrave Macmillan.

Lyotard, J. F. (1984) *The Postmodern Condition: A Report on Knowledge.* (Bennington, G. and Massumi, B. trans.) Minneapolis: University of Minesota Press. Originally published as *La Condition Postmoderne: Rapport sur le Savoir* (1979) Paris: Les Éditions de Minuit.

Mackrell, J. (2012) Wendy Houstoun – Review. *The Guardian.* 14 October. [online]. Available from: http://www.theguardian.com/stage/2012/oct/14/wendy-houstoun-review [Accessed 10 October 2013].

Mangan, M. (2013) *Staging Ageing: Theatre, Performance and the Narrative of Decline.* Bristol: Intellect Books.

Mangelsdorff, L. (2002) *Kontakthof von Pina Bausch Getanzt von Damen und Herren ab 65.* Film. Berlin: Absolut Medien.

Martin, S. (2011) *Susi & Gabi's Salon.* [online]. Available from: http://www.susannemartin.de/category/salons/ [Accessed 7 September 2015].

Martin, S. (2012) Personal notes during the conference 'The Aging Body in Dance: Seeking Aesthetics and Politics of the Body through the Comparison of Euro-American and Japanese Cultures', Berlin, 28-30 June 2012, unpublished.

Martin, S. (2014) Personal notes during Rosi Braidotti's lecture 'Thinking as a Nomadic Subject', Berlin, 7 October 2014, unpublished.

McPherson, K. (2012) *Force of Nature.* Film. Naimshire: Goat Media. Trailer available from: https://vimeo.com/34894689 [Accessed 14 September 2015].

Melrose, S. (2007) *Confessions of an Uneasy Expert Spectator*. [online]. Available from: www.sfmelrose.org.uk [Accessed 12 July 2010].

Melrose, S. (2005) *Words Fail Me: Dancing with the Other's Familiar*. [online]. Available from: www.sfmelrose.org.uk [Accessed 13 September 2013].

Mezur, K. (2013) Critical Age Studies in Dance or Dancing Aging. *Documentation of Dance Congress 2013: Performing Translations*. [online]. Available from: http://www.tanzkongress.de/en/documentation/texts/reports.html [Accessed 12 December 2013].

Midgelow, V. (2007) *Reworking the Ballet: Counter-Narratives and Alternative Bodies. Abingdon*: Routledge.

Midgelow, V. (2012) Nomadism and Ethics in/as Improvised Movement Practices. *Critical Studies in Improvisation / Études Critiques en Improvisation*, 8 (1) [online]. Available from: http://www.criticalimprov.com/article/view/2001/2705. [Accessed: 13 January 2013].

Midgelow, V. (2013) Dance and the Academy: Improvisation, (Dis)appearance and Language. Lecture. Middlesex University London, 23 September 2013 [online]. Available from: https://www.youtube.com/watch?v=ku2x8nBslUk. [Accessed 12 December 2014].

Miller, J. G. (2007) *Ariane Mnouchkine: Routledge Performance Practitioners*. Abingdon: Routledge.

Morrish, A. (2013) *Untitled Solo*. [Berlin: ImprovisationXchange Berlin, Studio Frangenheim 1 August 2013].

Morrish, A. (2014a) *Artistic Response to Age(ing)*. [online]. Available from: https://vimeo.com/album/3144399/video/115800921. [Accessed 17 October 2016].

Morrish, A. (2014b) Interview with Author. [online]. Available from: https://vimeo.com/album/3144399/video/116460223. [Accessed 17 October 2016].

Morrish, A. (2015) website. Available from: http://www.andrewmorrish.com/ [Accessed 7 September 2015].

Nakajima, N. (2011) De-Aging Dancerism: The Aging Body in Contemporary and Community Dance. *Performance Research* 16 (3), pp. 100-104.

Nakajima, N. and Brandstetter, G. (eds.) (2016) *The Aging Body in Dance: A Cross-Cultural Perspective.* New York: Routledge. (forthcoming)

National Health Service UK (2013) *Dementia Guide.* [online]. Available from: http://www.nhs.uk/conditions/dementia-guide/pages/about-dementia.aspx [Accessed: 1 September 2013].

National Institute of Dance Medicine and Science UK (2013) website. Available from: http://www.nidms.co.uk/ [Accessed 20 September 2013].

Nelson, R. (ed.) (2013) *Practice as Research in the Arts: Principles, Protocols, Pedagogies, Resistances.* Basingstoke: Palgrave Macmillan.

Neuroplacticity Lab at Ruhr-University Bochum (2015) website. Available from: http://www.neuralplasticitylab.de/index.aspx?culture=EN [Accessed 7 September 2015].

Novack, C. J. (1990) *Sharing the Dance: Contact Improvisation in American Culture.* Madison: University of Wisconsin Press.

Novak Lindblad, B. (2015) website. Available from: http://bigwind.se/forestallningar/barn-unga/birollen-och-musikanten/ [Accessed 7 September 2015].

Ohno, K. and Ohno Y. (2004) *Kazuo Ohno's World From Without and Within.* Middletown: Wesleyan University Press.

Pallant, C. (2006) *Contact Improvisation: An Introduction to a Vitalizing Dance Form.* Jefferson: McFarland.

Parker-Starbuck, J. and Mock, R. (2011) Researching the Body in/as Performance. In: Kershaw, B. and Nicholson, H. (eds.) *Research Methods in Theatre and Performance.* Edinburgh: Edinburgh University Press. pp. 2010-235.

Peters, G. (2009) *The Philosophy of Improvisation.* Chicago: University of Chicago Press.

Platel, A. and van Laecke, F. (2010) *Gardenia.* Performance. [Berlin: HAU 1, 19 August 2010].

Post, S. G. (2014) In Response to Margaret M. Gullette. *Age Culture Humanities* 1 [online]. Available from: http://ageculturehumanities.org/WP/issue-1/ [Accessed 12 December 2014].

Pudelko, B. (2010) *Alte Liebe*. Performance. [Berlin: Dock 11, 26 November 2010].

Rainer, Y. (2006) *Feelings are Facts: A Life*. Cambridge: MIT Press.

Rainer, Y. (2014) The Aching Body in Dance. *PAJ: A Journal of Performance and Art* 36 (1), pp. 3-6.

Reuter, G. (2015) website. Available from: http://www.gabrielereuter.de/ [Accessed 7 September 2015].

Riviere, J. (1929) Womanliness as Masquerade. *International Journal of Psychoanalysis* 10, pp. 303-313. [online]. Available from: http://de.scribd.com/doc/38635989/Riviere-Joan-Womanliness-as-Masquerade-International-Journal-of-Psychoanalysis-Vol-10-1929-303-13#scribd [Accessed: 29 July 2015].

Ross, J. (2007) *Anna Halprin: Experience as Dance*. Berkley: University of California Press.

Rudstrøm, S. (2015) website. Available from: http://www.stenrudstrom.com/ [Accessed 7 September 2015].

Ryle, G. (2009) *The Concept of Mind*. Sixtieth Anniversary Edition. Abingdon: Routledge.

Schön, D. A. (1983) *The Reflective Practitioner: How Professionals Think in Action*. New York: Basic Books.

Sandelowski, M. and Barroso, J. (2002) Finding the Findings in Qualitative Studies. *Journal of Nursing Scholarship* 34 (3), pp. 213-220.

Satin, L. (1999) Autobiography in the Present Tense: Deborah Hay, Living and Dying At Once. *Women & Performance* 10 (1-2), pp. 181-210.

Schwaiger, E. (2005a) Performing One's Age: Cultural Constructions of Aging and Embodiment in Western Theatrical Dancers. *Dance Research Journal*, 37 (1), pp. 107-120. [online]. Available from: http://www.jstor.org/stable/20444622 [Accessed 10 October 2011].

Schwaiger, E. (2005b) Sustainability in Dance Practice: The Case of the 'Mature Artist'. In: *Dance Rebooted: Initializing the Grid*. proceedings of a conference, Melbourne, 2004. [online]. Available from: http://ausdance.org.au/articles/details/sustainability-in-dance-practice [Accessed 9 January 2013].

Schwaiger, E. (2006) To Be Forever Young? Towards Reframing Corporeal Subjectivity in Maturity. *International Journal of Ageing and Later Life* 1 (1), pp. 11-41. [online]. Available from: www.ep.liu.se/ej/ijal/2006/v1/i1/a2/index.html [Accessed 6 July 2010].

Schwaiger, E. (2009) Performing Youth: Ageing, Ambiguity and Bodily Integrity. *Social Identities* 15 (2), pp. 273-284.

Schwaiger, E. (2012) *Ageing, Gender, Embodiment and Dance: Finding a Balance*. New York: Palgrave Macmillan.

Scolieri, P. (2012) Rhythms of Resurrection: The Comebacks of Ruth St. Denis. *Women & Performance* 22 (1), pp. 89-107.

Segal, L. (2014) The Coming of Age Studies. *Age Culture Humanities* 1. [online]. Available from: http://ageculturehumanities.org/WP/issue-1/ [Accessed 12. December 2014].

Silke Z. (ed.) (2014) *Unter Uns! Künstlerische Forschung, Biographie, Performance*. Bielefeld: Transcript.

Simson, K. (2013) Interview with Author. [online]. Available from: https://vimeo.com/album/3144399/video/117787682. [Accessed 17 October 2016].

Sontag, S. (1972) The Double Standard of Aging. *Saturday Review* 55, pp. 29-38.

Stark Smith, N. (2003) Life Scores. In: Albright, A. C. and Gere, D. (ed.) *Taken by Surprise: A Dance Improvisation Reader*. Middletown: Wesleyan University Press. pp. 245-254.

Stoller, S. (ed.) (2014) *Simone de Beauvoir's Philosophy of Age: Gender, Ethics, and Time*. Berlin: Walter de Gruyter.

Stubblefield, E. and Halprin, A. (1997-2000) *Still Dance with Anna Halprin*. [online]. Available from: http://www.stilldance.net/StilldanceAnna01.htm [Accessed 14 September 2015].

Stuve, O. (2015) website. Available from: http://dissens.de/gerenep/english.php [Accessed 7 September 2015].

Sullivan, S. (2000) Reconfiguring Gender with John Dewey: Habit, Bodies, and Cultural Change. *Hypatia*. 15 (1), pp. 23-42.

Swinnen, A. and Stotesbury J. A. (eds.) (2012) *Aging, Performance and Stardom: Doing Age on the Stage of Consumerist Culture*. Berlin: Lit.

Swinnen, A. (2013) Van Stereotiepe Beeldvorming naar Dementievriendelijk Samenleven. In: Hendriks, R., Hendrikx, A., Kamphof, I., Swinnen, A. *Delen in Dementie: Onderzoeksreflecties.* Maastricht: University Maastricht. pp. 12-17.

Tamed Organisation für Tanzmedizin (2015) website. Available from: http://www.tamed.de/ [Accessed: 1 September 2013].

Theater M21 (2015) website. Available from: http://joachimvonburchard.de/arbeiten.html [Accessed 7 September 2015].

Thomas, H. and Cooper L. (2002) Dancing Into the Third Age: Social Dance as Cultural Text – Research in Progress. *Dance Research* 20 (1), pp. 54-80.

Thomas, H. (2013) *The Body and Everyday Life: A New Sociology.* Abingdon: Routledge.

Tompkins, M. (2003) *Song and Dance.* Performance. [Berlin: Haus der Berliner Festspiele, August 2003].

Tompkins, M. (2015) website. Available from: http://www.idamarktompkins.com/?q=en/marktompkins [Accessed 7 September 2015].

Turner, B. S. (1994) The Postmodernisation of the Life Course: Towards a New Social Gerontology. *Australian Journal on Ageing* 13 (3), pp. 109-111.

Uhlig D. (2012) *Come Back.* Performance. [Berlin: HAU 2, 20 March 2013].

Vandenhole, W., Desmet, E., Reynaert, D., Lembrechts, S. (eds.) (2015) *Routledge International Handbook of Children's Rights Studies.* New York: Routledge.

Wainwright, S. and Turner, B. S. (2006a) 'Just Crumbling to Bits'? An Exploration of the Body, Aging, Injury and Career in Classical Ballet Dancers. *Sociology* 40 (2), pp. 237-255.

Wainwright, S., Williams, C., Turner, B. S. (2006b) Varieties of Habitus and the Embodiment of Ballet. *Qualitative Research* 6 (4), pp. 535-558.

Waite, B. (2015) website. Available from: http://brendawaite.blogspot.de/ [Accessed 7 September 2015].

Waki J. (2015) website. Available from: http://www.bodytalkonline.de/ [Accessed 7 September 2015].

Wengraf, T. (2001) *Qualitative Research Interviewing: Biographic Narrative and Semi-Structured Methods*. Thousand Oaks: Sage.

West, C. and Zimmerman D. H. (1987) Doing Gender. *Gender & Society* 1 (2), pp.125-151.

Woodward, K. (1991) *Aging and Its Discontents: Freud and other Fictions*. Bloomington: Indiana University Press.

Woodward, K. (ed.) (1999) *Figuring Age: Women, Bodies, Generations*. Bloomington: Indiana University Press.

Woodward, K. (2002) Against Wisdom: The Social Politics of Anger and Aging. *Cultural Critique* 51, pp. 186-218.

Woodward, K. (2006) Performing Age, Performing Gender. *Feminist Formations* 18 (1), pp. 162-189.

World Health Organisation (2014) *Definition of an Older or Elderly Person*. [online]. Available from: http://www.who.int/healthinfo/survey/ageingdefnolder/en/ [Accessed 24 September 2014].

Zambrano, D. (2013) website. Available from: www.davidzambrano.org [Accessed: 1 September 2013].